HIS MAJESTY'S THEATRE

Proprietor : Joseph Benson : Lessees : Grossmith & Malone, Ltd.
LICENSEES & MANAGERS : GEORGE GROSSMITH & J. A. E. MALONE

PROGRAMME

of the

First Performance in English

of

JAMES ELROY FLECKER's

Poetic Prose Play

"HASSAN"

*Arranged for Production on
the Stage by BASIL DEAN*

The Play presented by
GEORGE GROSSMITH *and* J. A. E. MALONE
by arrangement with ReandeaN

FLECKER AND DELIUS —
THE MAKING OF 'HASSAN'

*This edition of 'Flecker and Delius' first published
1978 by Thames Publishing*

Printed by John G Eccles Printers Ltd, Inverness

ISBN 0 905210 06 9

FLECKER and DELIUS

— the making of 'Hassan'

DAWN REDWOOD

Thames Publishing
14 Barlby Road, London W10 6AR

CONTENTS

The front and back end-papers show pages from the programme of the 1923 London production.

PREFACE

822
F62h4r
cop.2

Music

This monograph is an extension of two articles published in the *Delius Society Journal* in January and April 1976, entitled 'Flecker, Dean and Delius: The History of *Hassan*', and of a talk given to the Delius Society in January 1977 entitled 'Flecker and Delius'.

ACKNOWLEDGMENTS

My thanks are due to many people who have given their help so readily, and I trust I have remembered to thank them personally. In particular I owe my thanks to Mr Basil Dean for his co-operation, which enabled me to have access to his correspondence and other material from the Basil Dean Collection, housed in the Northern District Library of Toronto. The first volume of his autobiography (*Seven Ages*, Hutchinson, 1970) provided useful material.

My grateful thanks are also extended to Mr John Sherwood, who not only allowed me to use extracts from his biography of Flecker (*No Golden Journey*, Heinemann, 1973) but gave me a great deal of help in other ways.

Dr Oswald Bill, of the Hessische Landes- und Hochschulbibliothek at Darmstadt, assisted by providing the review from the *Darmstädter Tagblatt* of 2 June 1923.

Mr Robert Threlfall, Musical Adviser to the Delius Trust, has provided valuable advice in respect of the music. Dr Lionel Carley, Archivist to the Delius Trust, helped by making certain letters and books available to me. Mr Stephen Lloyd has contributed material and advice. Fräulein Evelin Gerhardi, along with Mr John Green, assisted with the German translation of the reviews. Mr Malcolm Walker contributed his time to my research. Messrs Boosey and Hawkes made access to the musical scores possible. Mr Fred Tomlinson kindly offered assistance with the aspects dealing with Philip Heseltine. I am grateful to Mr Stephen Parry for numerous observations concerning Flecker, and to Mrs Olga Norden (née Nicholls) for making available her father's papers. She must be one of the few remaining English people to have seen the production at Darmstadt. I also wish to thank the Delius Trust for valuable assistance, and for permission to quote from letters in its possession. Last, but by no means least, I thank my husband, who gave me a great deal of support.

Dawn Redwood
October 1977

Chapter 1
THE BACKGROUND

'. . . one morning in the autumn of 1913 the greatest prize of all came my way. The bulky package had all the appearance of being just one more of those voluminous outpourings that it was part of my lot to read. With it there was a hastily scribbled note from Viola saying: "Please give this wonderful play special attention; we wanted Daddy to read it but he says it's too long." The play was *Hassan* by James Elroy Flecker.'[1]

Thus did Basil Dean recall his first encounter with *Hassan* nearly 60 years after the event.

Dean was born in 1888. After an abortive start to a career in the City, Dean the actor first walked the boards in 1906. During this spell of acting he quickly learned to take an interest in and learn the rudiments of stage management, the technician's job and all the other branches of theatrical work.

After working with Miss Horniman[2] a period of unemployment followed around 1910, after which fairytale magic took him to Liverpool, where he collaborated with Miss Darragh[3] to form an experimental season, with himself in charge of the search for new plays and players. It was during this time that he began his close collaboration with many of the well-known playwrights of the period.

The critics' reception of Galsworthy's *Strife*,[4] chosen to open the season, made it clear that Basil Dean had established himself in the theatre. By November 1911 the experimental theatre had a home in Liverpool, and it was during this period that Dean met George Harris, '. . . an artist-craftsman of the highest quality, who was to become my closest friend and collaborator in the years ahead.'[5]

Dean soon made a name for himself as a producer who brought colour and vitality to the sets and imagination to lighting effects, and George Harris was able to realise Dean's ideas in his designs. Dean claimed that *Hassan* was the epitome of 'total theatre' for him and that his production was the only perfect opportunity to exercise his ideals.[6]

When Dean's days at Liverpool were over, Sir Herbert Tree[7] offered him the post of assistant producer at his theatre: at last Dean was part of London's theatrical life. Part of his job involved reading new plays to Tree. With Viola Tree's[8] words of advice ringing in his ears — '. . . Daddy is out of touch with new things in the theatre. You must give him new ideas and all that,'[9] Dean found the bulky package, already referred to, in December 1913.

Flecker was born in 1884, the son of a schoolmaster, and he lived and was educated in the home environment during his formative years. His father was headmaster of Dean Close School, Cheltenham, and his mother, the dominant parent, managed the domestic running of the school. His home and school life were synonymous with a very strict religious upbringing — so strict that normal boyish behaviour was severely reprimanded and any aesthetic or artistic traits in his personality were strongly discouraged. Mrs Flecker wrote of her son's upbringing:

> '. . . Frankly it was not a success. He was far too individualistic, far too egotistical to mix happily with the normal boy life of a public school, and he was very sensitive to the fact of being the Headmaster's son. Passionate and lacking in self-control, he was a trial to his masters since he could not take rebuke in any form, and his hastiness, inaccuracy and carelessness often got him into trouble.
>
> Roy always had the ability to work where his interests were engaged, but no power to endure what was irksome . . . Very early he began to be of the opposition, finding no doubt more scope for himself than along orthodox lines of discipline. From the letters of many who knew him at this time, it is obvious that though impressing people as a boy of real ability he did not display any "genius". Had he done so it might have been easier for him for he doubtless needed individual treatment.'[10]

Dr Flecker was overkeen for him to be an academic success, and the fact that his son not only wanted to write but could make a success of it was never reconciled with the parents' aspirations for him or with their religious views. Disagreement over religion and money were the two causes of all the friction between them. Never could Roy accept their narrow religious views, and when he became an agnostic he dealt the worst blow, in every possible dramatic way, to his parents.

Money was the joint cause of all the trouble, partly because he could not manage it (according to his parents) and partly because he spent his allowance on books and other allied tools of the artistic trade which were taboo to those strictly adhering to their religious principles. The disagreements continued (and much unhappiness they caused to all three), even to deathbed recriminations and absolutions.

After Dean Close and Uppingham, Flecker went up to Oxford, where he not only met many unsuitable characters — in his parents' eyes — but only just managed to gain a third in classics. With no particular career in mind, except an ambition to write, he enrolled in the Levant Consular Service and went on to Cambridge to study oriental languages, with a view to working as an interpreter. He chose this course at Cambridge partly because his two years of study would cover those aspects of literature he had acquired a taste for and partly because he could continue with his writing. He did write a lot of poetry, some of which was influenced by his study of the oriental style, and parts of *Hassan* date from this period.

On 23 April 1908 he enrolled as a 'student interpreter in His Majesty's Consular Service in the Ottoman Dominions, Persia, Greece and Morocco.' He was still only a student who had examinations to pass and these would always be irksome as they were invariably not on his favourite subject, and interrupted his own writing or research. These two years at Cambridge were not entirely happy and already he had felt the beginnings of the disease which was to prove fatal.

In June 1910, having gained fourth place out of the six candidates, he left Cambridge and headed for his first post in Constantinople — a place which was regarded by many in the service to have a poor climate and a narrow society.[11] However, the outward journey was a happy one, for it was on the boat that he met Hellé Skiadaressi,[12] whom he was to marry in 1911.

Hellé was an extremely well-educated Greek lady whose knowledge and love of literature complemented Flecker's perfectly. She later proved to be not only a good wife and literary companion but a valuable amanuensis for her sick husband. Unfortunately she was hardly acceptable to Dr and Mrs Flecker. She was foreign, she was unknown, her religion was Greek Orthodox, and her prospective husband was barely earning enough to keep himself — much less a wife. During their courtship they wrote constantly, and Flecker never kept any details of his illness from her. It was, ironically, on the black-edged consulate paper used after the death of Edward VII that he wrote to his parents on 16 September 1910:

'. . . I am afraid as usual that I am going to be an awful nuisance to you and everybody else. To go straight to the point, the doctor has discovered germs of consumption in me. He says I must take sick leave and consult a specialist at once. It's the greatest shock I've ever had, I'm utterly miserable, but the doctor says I can get cured.'[13]

So with less than three months' consular service to his credit, a thin, sick Flecker left the Middle East to seek a cure at a sanatorium in the Cotswolds. However, a restlessness set in and in January 1911 he left the sanatorium early and set off for Paris — and Hellé. The artistic life of Paris could hardly be described as a good example of the six-months' travel in the open-air which the doctor ordered after his stay in the sanatorium!

In the spring, when his money ran out, Flecker returned to Beirut. One can see why his parents felt he had thrown away the chance of a cure at this point, and in future they gave support less spontaneously.

Flecker was prone to the typical extremes of mental attitude which are a common feature of the illness from which he was suffering, especially in the later stages. These contrasts of restlessness and calm, euphoria and melancholia, periods of literary activity before a barren one, had earlier been incorrectly interpreted by his parents as part of his trying nature.

However, during his Paris sojourn he had completed his first play, *Don Juan*[14], and was pleased with some early criticisms of it from publishers and managers, not least among them Shaw.[15]

By March, Flecker was in Constantinople and had written to Hellé with a proposal of marriage. During the following month the consumption was active again, and during the ensuing period of sick-leave he married Hellé in Athens, on 25 May 1911. The first few weeks of their married life were spent in Corfu and he embarked on another play which was to take many shapes before assuming its final form as the *Hassan* Dean produced in 1923.

During the subsequent period he yearned for the literary life of London, and when he received a letter from Edward Marsh,[16] Flecker began to think seriously of leaving the grim, hot Middle-East and returning to the cultural haven of London. Marsh had written to Flecker at Rupert Brooke's[17] suggestion, asking him to submit some poems for an anthology of Georgian poetry which Marsh was editing. Flecker, of course, was pleased to be included and his close association with Marsh began at this time.

In July 1912 Flecker failed his exams for the Vice-Consulate but was given nine months' reprieve in view of the time spent on sick leave. In October 1912 he decided to leave the Service providing he could find a good job in London. So the Fleckers departed in November: Hellé went first to her mother in Paris and Roy to London. He soon met Marsh and was promised that *Hassan* would be shown to Granville Barker[18] as soon as it was typed. With hopes for the play high, Flecker searched in vain for this 'good job'.

After Mr and Mrs Flecker junior had visited their seniors in Cheltenham, and with a refusal by the Foreign Office to grant him a transfer, Hellé went back to Paris to throw off a virus, and Flecker returned reluctantly to Beirut.

Marsh was interested enough in *Hassan* for Flecker to write him a technical letter in January 1913 about alterations to Act I, Scenes 1 and 2. Christopher Hassall, in his biography of Marsh, wrote that *Hassan* was to '. . . cause the patron almost more work than any other literary project he ever touched.'[19] Hellé, meantime, had written from Paris: '. . . I think the day *Hassan* is played you will have enough to do writing for the stage and that will be the best thing for you and we must never forget or neglect this possibility.'[20]

Ironically, almost crossing in the post, Flecker wrote to tell her that he had 'rotten news' of *Hassan*. Henry Ainley,[21] one of the leading actors of the day who had been persuaded by Marsh to read it, regarded it as 'not commercial'. 'It obviously will never be played in its present form.'[22] At this point a mood of despair came over him, and he wrote to Hellé: '. . . I don't want to die in Syria, alone', and to his 'damn parents' he wrote: '. . . What a fool I was to come back, I have missed all my chances.'[23]

When Hellé arrived in Beirut at the end of March, Flecker was in hospital. By now his parents realised the gravity of the situation and offered their son a house on the South Coast: an offer which his mother wished, in retrospect, had been made four months earlier.

By May a specialist had ordered Flecker to make the journey to Switzerland immediately, at the same time informing Hellé 'that there was no time to lose'. He went to a sanatorium at Leysin, and after a few days there Flecker felt well enough to write another long letter to Marsh which detailed his work on the play. This involved writing three more acts instead of the one he had planned.

He was obviously very ill at this point and Hellé, who was acting as his amanuensis, was undergoing all the emotional and physical strain that Jelka Delius was to experience later.

By 5 August 1913 the first complete version of the play emerged from the Leysin sanatorium. Even this achievement did not lift his spirits very high, for in December he wrote to his father: '. . . I have got so much to say to the world, and no one will let me say it. It was the only thing I had left and it has failed.'[24]

In the same month Viola Tree's husband had obtained *Hassan* from Marsh and her enthusiasm for the play was immediate. Dean realised its potential at once but was astute enough to resist the temptation of showing it to Tree until it was of 'actable length'. Instead, he contacted Flecker through Marsh and proposed an arrangement whereby *Hassan* would take this 'final dramatic shape'. The play would be described as 'by James Elroy Flecker, arranged for production upon the stage by Basil Dean.' Flecker wrote to Marsh:

'. . . I will not conceal from you that were I well and not in exile, I should think several times before accepting. I do not believe myself that *Hassan* needs more alteration than I suggested in the Scenario[25] and which I could make in a week if I were well, and also the stage manager's inevitable improvements. But as it is, I accept *unreservedly*, only insisting that he gets to work at once!'[26]

However, Flecker was so worried about the type of alterations Dean might make that he retracted his agreement the next day, but was persuaded by Marsh to sign it on 30 January 1914. '. . . I can't help it. He is Tree's adviser and will probably get Tree to play it: he will certainly get it played somehow,' Flecker wrote to Savery.[27]

It was not only *somehow* but *sometime* before Dean did get *Hassan* produced. But for Flecker time was against him, and a projected meeting with Dean in Locarno never took place. Flecker arranged to meet Dean there but he had to leave the Italian lakes quickly for the sake of his health and return to the mountain air. He asked Dean to go to Davos but as Dean was on honeymoon he felt that it would be impossible under the circumstances, so he wrote a secret note of regret to Flecker. In his own words Dean explained: '. . . I felt this was a decision a bride should not be asked to share. Had I recognised it as my last opportunity of seeing him alive I might have acted differently.'[28]

By May, Flecker had to resign from the Service and he wrote a pathetic note to Marsh: '. . . I find it hard to take an interest in *Hassan* now. I certainly shan't worry [Dean], in fact I only wish he could do all the work.'[29] This refers to the revisions that Flecker would carry out at Dean's suggestion. However, both men worked on revisions and, according to Dean, these crossed in the post.

During the summer of 1914, Dr Flecker's finances went through a bad patch and this weighed heavily on his son's mind. It is a pity Roy found out about them as he was prompted to write to Marsh: '. . . Honestly, I don't expect to trouble the face of the earth much longer, and as long as *Hassan* comes off I shall expire content.'[30] All his financial troubles would be over: he could repay the debt to his parents and, moreover, he would have proved his position as an established writer. But this was not to be: time was still against him. War broke out, ironically at about the same time that Marsh was able to tell Dean he had found a financial backer, to which Dean could only reply that such a prize as *Hassan* would be lost on the wartime stage and that everyone would have to wait until a post-war London could really do justice to such a marvellous play. A hint of Flecker's final pessimism permeates a letter home, written on 26 August 1914, in which he refers to the outbreak of war as having '. . . bust up all ideas of *Hassan* being played . . . Have had 8 months in bed now all but 7 days and feel I have no reason to go on living, being a burden to father and everyone else.'[31]

Time ran out for Flecker. The final cruel blow was dealt to his hopes when he died, aged 30, on 3 January 1915. He had written a prophetic letter about the play to his mother in the late autumn of 1913, again recorded by the same biographer: '. . . it is a masterpiece, but I shall never live to see it come into its own.'

His widow assured Dean ten years later that he would have liked the production.[32]

The third essential ingredient in the success of *Hassan* was the musical score specially written for it by Frederick Delius. Born Fritz Theodor Albert Delius on 29 January 1862, he was the fourth child of German immigrant parents who settled in Bradford. His father, a very successful wool merchant, ruled his family of 12 with Prussian severity, and Beecham later commented:'. . . It was fortunate for Frederick that he was blessed with a nature both cheerful and resilient, and was thereby able to endure with a greater equanimity than his brothers and sisters the repressive environment in which they were being raised.'[33]

He was educated at Bradford Grammar School and the International

College, Isleworth, after which he entered the family business. Successive trade-seeking missions to Stroud, Chemnitz, Norköpping and St. Etienne all began with rushes of commercial enthusiasm which were quickly followed by longer periods savouring the countryside and the musical delights of the nearest cultural centre. This led to a posting in the North of England, from which he was only able to escape by persuading his father to buy him the part-ownership of a Florida citrus farm.

Here once more the old pattern re-established itself: some six months of hard work were followed by a chance meeting with a music-teacher, who gave him an intensive training, and Delius was set up on his own as a teacher of music in America. It was eventually necessary for the family to hire a private detective to trace him and persuade him to return home. His father, who had always patronised music but simply did not consider the life of a musician suitable for his second son, was talked by Grieg[34] into allowing Frederick to study at Leipzig Conservatorium — a course which, in the event, the composer declared useless to him and left early.

With the help of a bachelor uncle resident in Paris he then embarked on a ten-year period in and around the French capital, during which time he worked assiduously at his art but without gaining more than a modicum of success.

In 1896 he meet Jelka Rosen,[35] a talented painter six years his junior. She was later to purchase a house with a splendid garden in the village of Grez-sur-Loing, and after a brief return visit to Florida, Delius joined her there, staying for the rest of his life. They married in 1903.

The first decade of the new century saw the recognition of Delius as a composer, first in Germany, and was also his period of most fruitful composition. There was but one blot on his happiness: some time during his Paris years he had contracted syphilis, a disease for which the only known 'cure' in those times merely cleared away the symptoms whilst driving the infection deep into the central nervous system. Years later it was to reappear with terrible results.

Beecham was worried about his health as early as 1910, when the composer attended the British première of *A Village Romeo and Juliet* at Covent Garden, and the same year saw the first of a regular series of visits to sanatoria at various European health-resorts.

By the time Dean first met him, in 1920, the fatal signs were already beginning to manifest themselves, and no doubt these were responsible for Hellé Flecker's description of the composer as related in Chapter 3. By the end of 1921, says Beecham, '. . . growing weakness, accompanied by pains in both arms and legs, increased rapidly.'[36] By 1923, when further music for the play was requested, he was unable to write and Jelka was acting as his amanuensis. In addition, he could only walk with the aid of two sticks, had to be carried up and down stairs, and spent most of his time in a wheel-chair. Total blindness followed, yet he remained as mentally alert as ever. Composition took a new lease of life with the arrival of Eric Fenby[37] in 1928. Delius died at Grez on 10 June 1934 and was later reinterred at Limpsfield, Surrey, on 24 May 1935.

FOOTNOTES

1. Basil Dean, *Seven Ages — An Autobiography 1888-1927* (Hutchinson 1970), p111. Viola was Sir Herbert Tree's daughter.
2. Miss Horniman (1860-1937): a theatre manager and patron who pioneered the modern repertory movement. She accepted Dean's first play, *Marriages are made in Heaven*, which he had to produce himself. Lewis Casson and Sybil Thorndike came together for the first time to act in the play; theirs was one of many famous acting partnerships for which Dean was responsible.
3. Miss Darragh: a colleague in Miss Horniman's company.
4. John Galsworthy, OM (1867-1933): novelist and dramatist of *The Forsyte Saga* and *The Skin Game*, to name only two.
5. Dean, *op cit*, p80. George Harris designed the scenery and effects for the 1923 *Hassan*.
6. *Ibid*, p182-3.
7. Sir Herbert Draper Beerbohm Tree (1853-1917): actor-manager of His Majesty's Theatre, which he had built in 1897.
8. Viola Tree (1884-1938): eldest daughter of above. Actress and singer. Married Alan Parsons, a dramatic critic, in 1912. It was through their friendship with Eddie Marsh that *Hassan* came to Dean's desk: '. . . On the 13 [December 1913], mindful of Flecker's interests [Marsh], arranged to meet Basil Dean at luncheon in the hope of persuading him to produce *Hassan*.' Marsh takes up his own story: '. . . I have given Flecker's play to Tree, and I'm really hoping that something may come of it. Basil Dean (. . . manager to Tree) thinks the world of it, so does Alan Parsons.' Christopher Hassall, *Edward Marsh — A Biography* (Longmans 1959), p254.
9. Dean, *op cit*, p104.
10. John Sherwood, *No Golden Journey* (Heinemann 1973), p9.
11. *Ibid*, p101. W D Peckham was an Oxford friend of Flecker's who had given him the idea of the Foreign Service two years previously. He wrote about 'the utter lack of society' outside the capital: 'All those men who have been a year or two in the country curse the service for that same reason.'
12. Hellé Skiadaressi (1882-1961).
13. Sherwood, *op cit*, p108.
14. *Don Juan* — Flecker's other play, posthumously published in 1925.
15. George Bernard Shaw (1856-1950): dramatist, critic and writer. He read the typescript of *Don Juan* and wrote a long letter, offering his opinion and advice to Flecker: 'There is no doubt in my mind that you have high qualifications for dramatic work.' Sherwood, *op cit*, p126. On reading *Hassan*, he said of one scene: '. . . This is the best thing of its kind since Shakespeare.' It was a letter which gave great satisfaction to the dying poet.
16. Edward Howard Marsh (1872-1953): literary correspondent and private secretary to Sir Winston Churchill. Founder and editor of *Georgian Poetry*.

[17] Rupert Brooke (1887-1915): a talented young poet, whose first volume of verse was published in 1911.

[18] Harley Granville Barker (1877-1946): author, actor and producer. A prominent member of the progressive theatre.

[19] Christopher Hassall, *Edward Marsh — A Biography* (Longmans 1959), p200-201. On the day Flecker met Marsh in order to show him Acts I and II, Flecker left the script at home and had to send it to Marsh.

[20] Sherwood, *op cit*, p168.

[21] Henry Hinchliffe Ainley (1879-1945): *The Oxford Companion to the Theatre* states that his appearance as Hassan was 'one of his finest'.

[22] Sherwood, *op cit*, p171-172.

[23] *Ibid*, p172.

[24] *Ibid*, p193.

[25] Late in 1913, Flecker wrote a scenario at Marsh's suggestion, hoping that Tree could be persuaded to read a summary of the play. Flecker put in his alterations, which he asked Marsh to show to Dean.

[26] Hassall, *op cit*, p265.

[27] Sherwood, *op cit*, p202. Frank Savery was a contemporary of Flecker's at Uppingham and later became his literary adviser and confidant.

[28] *Hassan*, Heinemann Drama Library Series (1951), noted in Dean's introduction.

[29] Sherwood, *op cit*, p203.

[30] *Ibid*, p211.

[31] Geraldine Hodgson, *The Life of James Elroy Flecker* (Blackwell 1925), p217.

[32] Dean, *op cit*, p189.

[33] Thomas Beecham, *Frederick Delius* (Hutchinson 1959), p18.

[34] Edvard Grieg (1843-1907): Norwegian composer who influenced Delius's style and encouraged his earliest compositions.

[35] Jelka Rosen (1868-1935): artist of considerable talent. A fluent linguist and widely read. She chose many of Delius's texts for him to set to music.

[36] Beecham, *op cit*, p190.

[37] Eric Fenby (b. 1906), professor of harmony at The Royal Academy of Music, London.

Chapter 2

JAMES ELROY FLECKER
and 'HASSAN'

Flecker will be remembered in the annals of literary history primarily as a poet: one who used words in a most exciting and original way. All the volumes published received favourable reviews, and several editions were reprinted. To summarise his position among the English poets of his era, I quote part of Rupert Brooke's obituary from *The Times* of 6 January 1915:

> '. . . His conversation was variegated, amusing and enriched with booty from the by-ways of knowledge. He was always and restlessly driven by his mind down such paths. He sought beauty everywhere, but preferred, for the most of his life, to find her decoratively clad. He loved England, Greece and the East, always with more passion than affection . . . His work gained in strength and clearness as he went on, and his craftmanship became singularly accurate.'

The Nation, which had published many of his poems, called him 'the most fastidious craftsman we have known since Tennyson'.[1]

Hassan is written in poetic prose. The play grew out of his love for the literature of the exotic east and it was subjected to many alterations and amendments before assuming its final shape. To trace its origins it is necessary to go back to 1909, for it was then that Flecker wrote *The War Song of the Saracens*. At the time he had no idea of placing it in a dramatic setting, but it slotted into place perfectly in the play at a later stage.

In May 1911 Flecker was on sick-leave and he had used the opportunity to get married. It was during his stay on Corfu a month later that he read a small book of farcical plays in Turkish. One of them was about 'the adventures of one Hassan, a simple and credulous man whose friends amused themselves by playing practical jokes on him with the aid of a Hebrew magician.' Flecker was not very hopeful for the future of *Don Juan*, and he became interested in writing another play. He sketched out a farce, based on the above idea, and added a female character named Yasmin. At the same time, he wrote the ghazel of the same name.

By now he had read Dr Mardrus's French translation of the *Arabian Nights* and consequently changed his setting from Turkey to Bagdad. He boldly called this his 'new Arabian Nights play — it will be more marvellously unsaleable and unstageable than anything ever written.'[2] He structured the play in three acts and on 25 July again informed Mavrogordato of the latest progress. His play had become:

'. . . an *Arabian Nights* Farce, entirely popular, to run ten thousand nights (or at least 1001); love, intrigue, ghosts, pageants, everything in Arabian-English prose.'[3]

In June he had also written a poem which is quoted here because its theme influenced the direction in which *Hassan* developed (although not until a year later).

THE GOLDEN JOURNEY TO SAMARKAND
PROLOGUE

We who with songs beguile your pilgrimage
    And swear that Beauty lives though lilies die,
We poets of the proud old lineage
    Who sing to find your hearts, we know not why, —

What shall we tell you? Tales, marvellous tales
    Of ships and stars and isles where good men rest,
Where nevermore the rose of sunset pales,
    And winds and shadows fall toward the West:

And there the world's first huge white-bearded kings
    In dim glades sleeping, murmur in their sleep,
And closer round their breasts the ivy clings,
    Cutting its pathway slow and red and deep.

II

And how beguile you? Death has no repose
    Warmer and deeper than that Orient sand
Which hides the beauty and bright faith of those
    Who made the Golden Journey to Samarkand.

And now they wait and whiten peaceably,
    Those conquerors, those poets, those so fair:
They know time comes, not only you and I,
    But the whole world shall whiten, here or there:

Widen those long caravans that cross the plain
    With dauntless feet and sound of silver bells
Put forth no more for glory or for gain,
    Take no more solace from the palm-girt wells.

When the great markets by the sea shut fast
    All that calm Sunday that goes on and on:
When even lovers find their peace at last,
    And Earth is but a star, that once had shone.

In July it was followed by an Epilogue, which was taken over without alteration for the end of his play. His 'Arabian Nights Farce' changed direction to a more serious play around the middle of 1912, a change that was a reflection of his own disenchanted views of the Middle East.

The poems referred to were first published in 1913 in an anthology entitled *The Golden Journey to Samarkand*. Flecker explained to Frank Savery in a letter written during July that:

> '. . . The Epilogue is the last scene of *Hassan* — or rather I wrote *Hassan* to lead up to the Epilogue. A moonlight scene, a sudden burst into poetry (you know my trick from *Don Juan*), and the singer with the beautiful voice is the character of the play — the famous singer Ishak . . . If it doesn't give the public shivers down the back when it is acted in its place, I'll never write again . . .
>
> '"Yasmin" is an anthology piece. It is part of *Hassan* — written for it and should sound well in its place.'⁴

The writing of *Hassan* spanned two years, and its journey through agents' and managers' hands occupied 18 months. The two processes took place concurrently because Flecker dispatched the first two acts of the play to London in July 1912. After he met Marsh[5] in November, he transferred the play to him, thinking that it would go further in his hands as Marsh was already handling a few of his poems for the anthology of *Georgian Poetry*. Marsh, of course, had good connections and his first offer of help was to show the play to Granville Barker. Marsh was sufficiently interested in the play to offer advice to Flecker, and the poet discussed technical details of his alterations in a letter to him on 2 January 1913:

> '. . . I honestly and without merely being amiable agree in your criticism. Indeed I am not at all sure about Act I, Scenes 1 and 2, but they might be exalted by making Hassan himself more exalted. I want to have plenty of buffoonery — but it should be universal. I hope you will tell anyone you send it to, not to despair till he reads past Act I, Scene 2. I shall have the 3rd Act ready in a month. I'll leave out the further magic scene that I had planned and try to give the beggars a better show.'⁶

Flecker's leave — and hopes for a job in England — expired on 3 January and a very dispirited and sick poet returned alone to Beirut. Another letter to Marsh followed, close on the heels of his last one:

> '. . . The hope of my life, which is *Hassan*, is in your hands, my dear Marsh. I am longing to hear what Ainley thinks of it, still more to hear what Barker hears [sic] of it, and no less to hear what you think of it. Do not scruple to tell me bad news and opinions. My best love to Rupert, and many thanks to you for your great kindness to one as unfortunate as Ovid.'⁷

However, when he received news of the play's prospects, it matched his pessimistic mood. He wrote to his wife in France on 12 February:

> '. . . Sorry to say I have rotten news of *Hassan*. Ainley regards it as "not commercial". It obviously will never be played in its present form. I agree with him [Marsh] about cutting out the farce. Shall write 3rd act after my exam.'⁸

Marsh, on the other hand, regarded the play very much as a commercial proposition; in fact he was a staunch champion of Flecker's cause.

In mid-May a specialist told Hellé that 'there was no time to lose' and sent Flecker to the sanatorium at Leysin in search of a cure for his tuberculosis. When he was able to work again, at the beginning of June, his thoughts turned immediately to *Hassan* and he wrote to Marsh, asking him to arrange for Drinkwater[9] to return the typescript of the first two acts. Apart from the fact that Drinkwater had kept the script for two months (which was far too long in Flecker's eye), he explained to Marsh the changes he would make when he wrote from Leysin on 6 June:

'. . . As life is beginning to stir within me and I've got nothing on earth to do but lie in bed all day feeling pretty well . . . I have determined to seize the opportunity, and finish and revise *Hassan*. I am going to cut the farce clean out — or modify it greatly, and be less heavy with the oriental expressions . . . It will be much better for Drinkwater and Barker to read my final version after all.'[10]

It is necessary, at this point, to explain that these first two acts of the play have subsequently come to be known as the First Version.[11] When Flecker began amending the play in June 1913 at Leysin, he altered parts of the plots and many aspects of the characters. All he had to do, as he explained himself, was write the third and final act. He did this between June and August, but he also wrote two more acts, thus having a play not only of five acts but one that was far too long for performance. Thus the Leysin Version superseded the First Version.

The play developed into five acts because Flecker enlarged the Rafi and Pervaneh story considerably. Rafi was in the First Version but his lost love and subsequent desire for revenge on the Caliph was only present in the form of a mention that Leila, a beautiful slave girl he loved and refused to sell, was seized for the Caliph's harem.

In Leysin, at the time he was completing the third act, a story[12] which Hellé had written for publication (but had been rejected) came to his mind as it had a theme which just fitted his play. The heroine chose death as an alternative to life with a lustful tyrant. Using this, Flecker could debate love and death, but there were drawbacks to the inclusion. It not only made the play very long but the emphasis on Hassan's character was reduced and altered slightly. Flecker appeared quite confident about his five-act play as he wrote to Savery on 5 July 1913:

'. . . I have got my *toy theatre* and play with it all day. I shall send you *Hassan* as soon as it is finished; I've still half an act to do. All my hopes are on it. It's utterly Oriental externally, but I hope the flash of the little European blood I possess gleams through its seraglio atmosphere from time to time!'[13]

At the beginning of August he finished the ghost scene and later told Hellé that it only took him half an hour to complete as he knew so clearly what he had to say. A month later he told Savery:

> '. . . The part of the play that thrills me most is the ghosts . . . I love my ghosts — I suppose because my poetic soul loves the picturesque in the play above everything.'[14]

All he had to do was stick a galley proof of the *Epilogue* on his manuscript, change the word 'Pilgrim' to 'Ishak' and alter 'make the Golden Journey' to 'take the Golden Road', as Marsh and others had persuaded him that the former did not scan.

Flecker did not give in to Marsh without a fight. On 25 July he claimed:

> '. . . I cannot — with all deference — get to like the "Golden Road" as much as the "Golden Journey": I wouldn't mind "Golden *Track*" so much.'[15]

But on 5 August he admitted defeat, for reasons which he explained to Marsh:

> '. . . The reviews have been few [referring to his recently published anthology entitled *The Golden Road to Samarkand*]. An excellent one in *The Globe* — but mentioning that he would prefer "Golden Road" to "Golden Journey" on account of the extra metric syllable. I bow to criticism and have just amended journey to road in the copy of the poem which ends the last act of *Hassan*.'[16]

The Leysin Version was subjected to many alterations before it was finally published by Heinemann in 1922 and even then it was not published with *exactly* all Flecker's alterations as written on the version at the Bodleian Library (see Appendix III), but all subsequent references to the play will be taken from the published edition by Heinemann in 1922.

All the leading characters are motivated by revenge. Once the plot has been introduced. Hassan threatens to wreak revenge on Selim and Yasmin for their cruel trick, for in the second scene of Act I he cries:

> 'I will have you both whipped through the city and impaled in the market-place, and your bodies flung to rot on a dung-heap . . . I will kill you.'

In the first scene of the second act, the theme of revenge is renewed in what was the sub-plot in earlier versions of the play but has now assumed an equal place with the Hassan story, for Rafi states his reasons to satisfy his revenge on the Caliph. The Caliph, of course, loses no time in taking his vengeance on Rafi and the Beggars. In the same way, the tables are turned on Hassan though, for the Caliph seeks vengeance for being labelled a 'hideous tyrant, torturer from Hell!'

Most of the characters have a cruel streak in their personality. Selim plays a school-boy trick on an innocent older man; Yasmin rejects Hassan and together with Selim delights in the trick that brought them together;

Rafi's revenge on the Caliph is justified, perhaps; Ali is cruelly beaten, while Yasmin takes a delighted, sadistic glance from her balcony; retaliatory cruelty pushes Hassan to the limit of his capabilities when, in Act III, Scene 2, he finds that Yasmin has been waiting for him.

Finally, there is the ultimate cruelty dictated by the Caliph in the Divan Scene, with its inevitable ending; first the beggars are led to death, followed by the prolonged agony of the trial. The Caliph delights in his sado-sexual offer to allow Rafi freedom if Pervaneh returns to his harem. He is further delighted to accommodate the torture scene in his Palace garden 'as a mark of favour' to Hassan and to 'have it held in his honour.'

There is the final cruelty of the torture scene, which Yasmin sadistically enjoys, for she admits she 'laughed to see them writhe'. The ghost scene ends that sequel in the play with the lovers' bleak statement on the futility of ideals, for the Ghost of the Earth cannot answer the play's key question and the Ghost of Pervaneh (she having chosen death in preference to a life of dishonour) can only cry 'Life is sweet'.

The Caliph is the central figure. He reigns supreme over the actions of the play, and although he dictates the drama he never takes part in the events themselves. Yasmin is closely associated with the sadistic undertones in the play very early on. She clearly casts a poisonous spell over Hassan which, try as he does, he cannot throw off. She asks him 'Are not my arms like swords of steel, hard and cold, and thirsty for blood?'

Yasmin shifts her fickle attention to anyone in power and she celebrates the end of the drama with Masrur. Rafi and Pervaneh provide the vehicle for Flecker to discuss life, love and death. Like Pervaneh, Ishak also has no cruel streak in his personality. The poet is a central figure in the play, but he stays in the shadow of the action and from there directs the play's transcendental mood. For the poet's mission in life is to debate on it, and it is through expression in poetry that he can attempt to alleviate the inevitable end to every soul's journey through life. Ishak put Hassan into the adventure, and he is there to rescue Hassan again from the fountain at the end of the play. It is Ishak who decides they shall take 'The Golden Road to Samarkand' in order to 'listen for the voice of the emptiness of earth'. In the final two scenes Ishak emerges from the shadows and takes Hassan away to join the Caravan. Flecker could not accept organised religion, but at this point in the play he strikes a positive note, for Hassan and Ishak leave to find 'the prophet who can understand why men were born.'

Hassan, the Confectioner, has fallen in love with Yasmin. He has no idea of the extent to which her insidious influence will affect him. He is an innocent man, lacking in active, cruel motives, and he becomes the instrument of other people's evil desires. When the drama has run its course and the fountain runs red, he turns his back on the cruelty and perversions and takes 'the Golden Road to Samarkand'. But he has to be led there, for when Ishak found him prostrate with horror after the torture scene, he pleaded 'Let me lie . . . This place is quiet, and the earth smells cool. May I never rise till they lift me aboard my coffin, and I'll go a sailing down the river and out to sea.'

Interwoven with the action are two symbols — the carpet and the fountain. The carpet is a constant reminder of Hassan's happy, simple life before he became involved in the drama. It is mentioned many times, literally and metaphorically. Hassan dreams 'Had I been rich, ah me!' But rebukes himself. '. . . But be content, O artist: thou has one carpet . . . thou hast one love'; but Hassan is not content because his love is unattained. When he is imprisoned with the Caliph in The House of the Moving Walls, he studies the 'ugliness of the pattern of this carpet' — a reflection of the ugly Rafi/Caliph revenge. When Ishak chooses to die as the penalty for deserting his master, 'the carpet of execution' is pinned to the sky. In Hassan's private apartment there is an 'an exquisite carpet. I have never seen so bright a scarlet.' This is the carpet on which the Caliph commands the lovers to be slain. When Hassan prepares to travel he chooses to take the 'old carpet that still lies in my shop' for he will stretch it out upon the desert when he says his evening prayers and it shall be 'a little meadow in the waste of sand'. The drama has run its full course, and Hassan returns to the safety and comfort of his old carpet, with which he is now content.

As a contrast to the earthly symbol of the carpet, there is the fountain; it is the focus of attention throughout, both because of its involvement in the action and on account of its symbolic function — the cleansing.

Hassan turns to the fountain for comfort and solace in the second scene of the play. Ishak was content — 'For me the break of day is adventure enough — and the water splashing in the fountain', but Hassan pursued his love, and it is only when the drama has run its full course, and the fountain has run red, that he can leave for the Pilgrimage.

The beautiful fountain in the Pavilion Garden was evilly acquired as the Caliph related to Hassan. Hassan, anguished to hear the story, cried 'O Fountain, dost thou never run with blood? . . . You have told a tale of death and tyranny, O Master of the World'.

The carpet and the fountain are used as a joint symbol when Hassan threatens Yasmin that 'your blood shall fall on my carpet' drop by drop, like the fountain. During the torture scene, the only sounds to be heard are the splashing of the fountain and the whirling of the wheel. Ishak finds Hassan beside the fountain, crazed with the horror of the scene.

Up to this point the fountain has witnessed the drama, but now it dictates the drama. It runs red and Ishak and Hassan flee in terror. The Fountain Ghost speaks clearly of life and death and of the futility of ideals. He cannot provide a satisfying answer to the riddle of death, and returns to the earth as the camel bells summon the Pilgrims.

Flecker's poetry is rich in colour and so expresses the strong symbolism of colours. Red is alluded to many times; in particular there is the red rose of love and later, when all that he aspired to turns against Hassan, the symbolic red of the burning agony of pain.

The stage directions use colour, especially red. There is the red glow for Ishak's proposed execution; the walls redden in the prison when the lovers announce their decision; and for the Procession of Protracted Death a 'deep red afterglow illumines the black garden'. Yasmin asks Hassan if her lips were not drenched in blood, to which he can forsee his own tragedy by answering, 'God, I shall fall!'

White is used with a somewhat spiritual effect. In Yasmin's poem, Hassan foretells the pale white ghosts, the prophet and the Golden Journey:

'. . . The morning light is clear and cold: I dare not in that light behold
A whiter light, a deeper gold, a glory too far shed, Yasmin.'

Here it is a *golden* journey, to contrast with the red referred to so many times in the play.

The Caliph was complimented by Ishak because to him 'Agony is a fine colour, and he delights therein as a painter in vermilion'. As he is the play's central force, every action in the play centres around his commands, and the central symbol — the fountain — had to run red, perhaps to cleanse the souls of those involved, in order to purge them of their involvement in the plot before they could set out on 'The Golden Road to Samarkand'.

To go further, the journey begins in darkness: a darkness to cover the sins of corruption before the dawn of a new day. It is with hopes for a golden ideal that will not tarnish that the Pilgrims set out.

FOOTNOTES

[1] Sherwood, *op cit*, p222.
[2] *Some Letters From Abroad of James Elroy Flecker* (Heinemann 1930), p46.
[3] *Ibid*, p48. John Mavrogordato, a reader for Dent's and editor of the *English Review*.
[4] *Ibid*, p98. Contrary to what Flecker explained to Savery, he did not have any plans to incorporate 'Yasmin' into his farce.
[5] Flecker sent the first act of *Hassan of Bagdad* to George Alexander but later gave the play to Marsh to manage.
[6] Sherwood, *op cit*, p166.
[7] *Ibid*, p166.
[8] *Ibid*, p171.

⁹ John Drinkwater (1882-1937): poet, dramatist, producer, actor and general manager. Hassall (*op cit*, p206) mentions that Granville Barker was too busy to read any new manuscripts and that Marsh proposed sending the fragment to John Drinkwater (son of A. E. Drinkwater, Barker's reader at Birmingham Repertory Theatre). But Flecker was adamant that the first production should be in London: 'Damn it, I'm ambitious' he admitted to Savery when discussing the subject.

¹⁰ Sherwood, *op cit*, p182-3.

¹¹ A typescript of Act I is at the University of Texas.

¹² Sherwood, *op cit*, p206.

¹³ *Some Letters From Abroad*, p93.

¹⁴ *Ibid*, p107.

¹⁵ *Ibid*, p94.

¹⁶ *Ibid*, p95.

Chapter 3

THE CHOICE OF COMPOSER

When London began to regain its cultural equilibrium after the First World War, most of those involved in pre-war theatre life had to start again on the bottom rung of the ladder. Among them was Basil Dean, who was perhaps luckier than some because he had been involved with the theatre as he organised entertainment for the troops. Nevertheless, a civilian job had to be found. Perhaps one might say the civilian job found him — in the middle of Piccadilly's traffic.

Dean had been lunching with his pre-war friend Alec Rea[1] and prior to saying good-bye Rea asked his friend what he would be doing when the war was over. Dean made no firm reply — he did not have one to make — and Rea then proposed that he would finance a new theatrical company. With a 'Think it over and let me know'[2] Rea disappeared into the traffic.

Dean hardly needed any persuading, but much hard work had to be put into the formation of this new company. The conglomerate name of *ReandeaN* was chosen, and past as well as new associates were invited to join, among them George Harris and E P Clift.[3]

St. Martin's Theatre was their home, but it had one disadvantage, as Dean was to find out later: its stage was not large enough to suit his ideas for *Hassan*. That problem was solved in time, but first Dean contacted Mme. Flecker and told her of the newly-formed company.

She came to London in June 1919 and they began their discussions of the long-awaited production. Mme. Flecker was expecting the play to be produced that autumn: not a very practical expectation in view of the fact that London was recovering from the effects of war, and that the play was no mean undertaking.

Flecker had stated that 'an oriental play must be a spectacle of course', and Dean hoped and intended to make it one. To appease Mme. Flecker, Dean's agent drew up an agreement that was to secure him the dramatic rights for twelve months in exchange for an advance royalty payment. However, the ensuing delay over the production gave rise to a long 'diplomatic and undiplomatic'[4] correspondence between them.

By this time Dean had begun to think seriously about the production, and one of the major gaps to be filled was music. The poet had always wanted music,[5] and while Dean admits he had no musical knowledge ('only a great love of it'), he knew exactly what he wanted and where it should occur.

The first mention of music in their correspondence appears in a letter dated 13 December 1919. Mme. Flecker writes:

> '. . . I should be much obliged if you would let me know, when you tackle the play, what your plans about the music would be, as I know one or two composers who would be glad to write the music if you have not already promised the musical part to anyone.'

Whatever Dean replied, no progress was made for several months, and Mme. Flecker became so exasperated that the following April she threatened to take the play elsewhere if ReandeaN did not produce it very soon.

Dean went to Paris, again to appease her, and on his return to London the real correspondence over the choice of composer began. As it does not indicate who made the first suggestion — that of Ravel[6] — one can only assume that it was made verbally during their recent meeting and by Mme. Flecker. Dean began their correspondence on 14 May 1920:

> '. . . Would you get into touch with Maurice Ravel and ascertain whether there would be any possibility of his doing the music of "HASSAN". I think it would be desirable for him to begin working on it immediately.'

But not waiting for her reply, Dean wrote again on 19 May 1920:

> '. . . I have wired you this day as follows: "Ducasse[7] suggested for Hassan music is he in Paris if so see him" — Dean.
>
> I am told that Ducasse is a young French composer whose work might be of sufficient calibre for "HASSAN". I regret I do not know his work and I am wondering if you do. If you do, perhaps you would get into touch with him on the subject. Since writing you I have heard of an English composer whom I think could do the work. His name is Harold Samuel.[8] He would, I believe, be willing to do it but I should not know until about 2 June. He was the man I originally thought of but he was so busy on other work that he told me he would not have time. He now thinks he could manage it. I think you will agree with me that it would be desirable to have the music done by an Englishman if possible.'

Mme. Flecker replied on 20 May that:

> '. . . I had already written to Maurice Ravel so that I better wait for his answer before seeing Ducasse who I believe is in Paris. I cannot say if Ravel can tackle the music immediately as he is always very busy but I do believe he is much the more suitable of the two for "Hassan".'

She wrote again on 26 May to say:

> '. . . I have had an answer from Maurice Ravel who is in the country. He says he is very busy but is very much interested and wants to know exactly how much work the music for "Hassan" represents and the date of production so as to decide if he can undertake it. I have written to him today and so as not to loose [sic] time waiting for your answer to this I have given him the following list of necessary music . . . Please let me know if you agree. As for the date I told him not before December. He will be

coming to Paris for a few days soon when I shall be able to see him but I shall probably get an answer before that so I should be obliged if you take no engagement with other composers before you hear from me. I do believe Ravel would do his best and as he is very fashionable just now his name would certainly add to the chances of success.'

To which Dean replied, on 31 May, in business-like tones, that he agreed with her suggestions for music but '. . . of course there will have to be the closest co-operation between myself and the composer . . .'

He thought the play might be produced in November, but as he would shortly be visiting Paris with his designer (George Harris), this would be a favourable opportunity to meet Ravel, though of course '. . . I should have to have his definite answer and some form of business understanding with him before then.'

Mme. Flecker's next letter, of 1 June, was not so optimistic as Ravel had replied to say that '. . . he cannot possibly undertake such an important work if it is to be ready next December.' Although she asked Dean to let her know the 'furthest date' for which the music was to be completed, she ended '. . . if you have by now received a favourable answer from Mr Samuel I can of course tell Ravel you cannot give him more than 6 months time.'

These two letters crossed in the post, so she confirmed that she would wait for Dean's 'furthest date' in her next letter, of 2 June. She went on to mention another suggestion which again must have first been put forward at their recent meeting, that '. . . perhaps your idea of having a choice of Russian music could be followed?'

Dean's reply of 3 June shows a hint of exasperation with Ravel. If he couldn't deliver the music by December '. . . then by what date could he have the music ready?' Dean had other ideas. He continues '. . . I have already another composer of first-rate quality who has been suggested, and that is Arnold Bax.[9] I am proposing to get into touch with him immediately.' He ends on a more constructive note, though, as '. . . we have given the designer instructions to get forward with the work of designing the scenery and costumes.'

Mme. Flecker did not abandon her hopes for Ravel, but there is a mood of pessimism. She tells Dean on 9 June:

'. . . I am writing to ask Mr Ravel what would *his* date be for having the music ready. I fear he will ask for a very long delay as he is busy on an opera[10] so I think you better not wait for his answer but get in touch with whoever you think could do the job among the English composers. I have heard much praise of Norbert Howells[11] [sic] (Royal College of Music) whom many consider a genius. Personally I know nothing of his music. I wonder though if a selection of Russian or perhaps of *old Italien* [sic] music, Pergolese[12] [sic] or Cimarosa[13], would not be a better plan if we cannot have a composer with a name like Ravel's that looks well on the programme whether his music be suitable or not, which very few people can tell. I believe Mr Edward Dent[14] who is very learned both in old Italian and in modern Russian music could be applied to for such a selection.'

On 11 June of that year (1920) the name of Frederick Delius appears for the first time among the nine composers considered for the commission. Dean writes:

'. . . I shall not wait for Monsieur Ravel's answer. Already I am making some enquiries to see whether Frederick Delius, whose music I know and greatly admire, would do the work for us. He recently composed the opera "A VILLAGE ROMEO AND JULIET"[15] which was done by Sir Thomas Beecham[16] at Covent Garden, and was an enormous success. I have myself thought of the possibility of having a selection of existing music made. But there is this difficulty, that as I desire to have Hassan's poem to Yasmin in Act I intoned to music and also the whole of the last scene of the play played to music, I consider that it would be extremely difficult to find the right piece of music at the right rhythm to suit the words.'

Dean described his encounter with *A Village Romeo and Juliet* in his autobiography. He had been working late with George Harris on designs for *Hassan* — it must have been 19 or 24 March or 10 April — and their walk home took them past Covent Garden:

'. . . I had recently read a notice of this little-known opera and, on a sudden impulse, persuaded George to come in and listen to it. We crept into the back of a box and soon found ourselves immersed in the glorious music of "The Walk to the Paradise Garden". Never had I heard such a fountain of sound. I was enthralled. I turned to George and said: "This is the man I want for "HASSAN". I wrote off the next day to Mme. Flecker and told her that I was not going to wait any longer for Ravel's decision. I had made up my mind. I wanted Frederick Delius.'

It is now clear from Dean's letter of 11 June that he did not 'write off the next day' as he claims but waited until their correspondence over the choice of composer began and so again he wrote on 17 June:

'. . . I have now got quite the best suggestion possible I think for the composer of "HASSAN". It is Frederick Delius. I understand that he is in France and that his address is:

Crez-sur-Loing [sic]
Seine et Marne.

As I am going over to Paris about the 12th or 13th of next month, I think I had better try and get into touch with him on this matter as there is no time to be lost. He is quite the best suggestion we have had so far, and I am very keen to secure his co-operation . . .

If you know anybody of influence who knows Delius it might be as well to get them to speak to him about the subject of "HASSAN". If, however, you don't, it would perhaps be best for me to approach him in the ordinary business way. Will you let me know if you are doing anything in the matter?'

Mme. Flecker replied on 21 June:

'. . . I don't know anyone who could speak to Mr Frederick Delius. I think you better write to him directly and tell him I could give him the details of the question if he likes and then you could see him in July when you are over here . . . Ravel writes he could not know before the end of July if he could undertake the music for 'Hassan' and by what date he could have it ready next year; besides he does not know English which is a drawback. I do hope Fred. Delius will be able to do the job. But I believe you must lose no time; modern music takes a very long time to be written.'

It would appear that Dean was the first to visit Delius — on 15 July — for on the previous day Delius wrote to Philip Heseltine:

'. . . I am receiving the visit of a Mr Basil Dean of the St. Martin's Theatre tomorrow. He wants to show me a play!! Who is he?'

Dean described this visit in his autobiography:

'. . . I decided to go to France to see the composer and to take Harris with me. From Paris we set out for Grez-sur-Loing. It was a sunny day in July, a day of pictures in the memory: the village street was quiet in the summer's heat, then the clanging bell while we waited at the door of the villa; in the cool interior Mme. Delius, a tall, gracious hostess, waiting to give us luncheon and, after coffee in the lovely walled garden, to show us her pictures. Above all, there remains the vivid impression of the Maestro himself. Delius was unlike the popular idea of a composer. His thin, aesthetic face and precise diction suggested a professor, perhaps of philosophy, rather than a musician, while his faint North Country accent and brisk manner hinted at business training. We went through the play together, Delius agreeing without demur to the amount of music I required and the places where it should occur.'[17]

Mme. Flecker then made contact with the composer and after she received Jelka's travel instruction she made her way to Grez, as she relates in her next letter to Dean, on 27 July:

'. . . I had a long talk with Mr Fr. Delius the other day about 'Hassan'. He seems rather worried about the extremely reduced numbers of the orchestra you can afford him . . .[18] I think Mr Delius is anxious to do the music for the play and judging from his appearance — a bundle of quivering and spasmodic nerves — he is probably a very good musician so that I believe it could be worthwhile securing him, especially as time is so short and he seems willing to have most of the music ready by December.'

Hellé had obviously noticed the early signs of Delius's affliction, as did Dean during his visit:

'. . . [his] mind was alert and his views decisive even though the disease that was eventually to destroy [him] had already begun to show itself.'[19]

Dean replied promptly on 29 July:

'. . . I think it will be quite impossible to have an orchestra of 30 musicians for "HASSAN" . . . I have promised Mr Delius 21 musicians . . . The trouble of course is that Mr Delius is accustomed more to Operatic work where an orchestra of 60 is nothing. If he is unable to take up the work I am assured that Mr Rutland Boughton[21] would undoubtedly suit our purpose equally well and probably be more accessible. In fact many of my musical friends who are the up-to-date coming authorities on music tell me that he would be a wiser choice, as being a younger man and more amenable to ideas. I have not had an answer from Mr Delius with reference to my last letter in which I suggested terms. I am wondering if you could take up the matter tactfully and get a decision. I have good reason for saying that, should he refuse to do the music, it might not be to our disadvantage, but of course I cannot say more in this letter.'

Dean's final letter in that sequence, written on 24 August, strikes a more positive note:

'. . . I think you would like to know that I have finally settled up things with Mr Delius . . . the production will probably take place some time during the first three months of the New Year.'

FOOTNOTES

[1] Alec Rea: an early colleague of Dean's and wartime chairman of the Liverpool Playhouse.
[2] Dean, *op cit*, p129.
[3] E P Clift: manager of the latest garrison theatre at Catterick Camp and later Dean's business manager. He negotiated Dean's agreement with Delius for *Hassan*.
[4] Dean, *op cit*, p181.
[5] *Ibid*, p144. '. . . The poet had always wanted music, not only for the songs and ballets, but specifically to accompany the poem at the end: "The Golden Road to Samarkand",' radio broadcast given by Basil Dean, 3 July 1968.
[6] Maurice Ravel (1875-1937): French composer and pupil of Fauré who studied at the Paris Conservatoire.
[7] Jean Roger-Ducasse (1873-1954): French composer who was also a pupil of Fauré. He completed Debussy's *Rhapsody for saxaphone and orchestra*.
[8] Harold Samuel: a friend of Basil Dean. An English pianist who did much arranging, particularly of the music of Bach. Dean, *op cit*, p150.
[9] Arnold Bax (1883-1953): composer, influenced by Irish literature and folk-lore. Master of the King's Music 1941-1953.
[10] *L'Enfant et les Sortilèges*.
[11] Herbert Howells (b. 1892): sometimes known as Norman. English composer, a pupil of Stanford; teacher and cathedral organist.
[12] Giovanni Pergolesi (1710-1736): Italian composer, violinist and church organist. Wrote serious and comic operas.
[13] Cimarosa (1749-1801): Italian composer of 60 operas.
[14] Edward Joseph Dent (1876-1957): musicologist, Professor of Music at Cambridge. He was also a friend of Delius.
[15] *A Village Romeo and Juliet*: Delius's best-known opera, composed in 1900-1.
[16] Sir Thomas Beecham (1879-1961): English conductor and founder of London Philharmonic Orchestra. Founder and conductor of Royal Philharmonic Orchestra 1946. Friend and champion of Delius.
[17] Dean, *op cit*, p145-6.
[18] See Chapter 6 for detailed account.
[19] Radio broadcast given by Dean, 3 July 1968.
[20] It will be seen from the dates of these letters just what a first-class postal service there was in those days!
[21] Rutland Boughton (1878-1960): English composer, conductor and writer. He organised a Festival Operatic Centre at Glastonbury 1914-1925.

Chapter 4

PARALLELS BETWEEN FLECKER AND DELIUS

There is no evidence to suggest that Flecker and Delius ever met. Nevertheless, their paths ran in close approximation at certain times, and in view of the complementary nature of their work it is instructive to follow these parallels.

Their lives

1 Neither man was of English origin: three of Flecker's grand-parents were Polish Jews and Delius's parents were German.

2 Both men had inflexible and authoritarian fathers.

3 Both sets of parents had taken active steps to prevent their sons embarking on what they considered to be unsuitable careers.

4 As a result of their son's determination to go ahead, neither Flecker's nor Delius's parents supported their son's choice. They further demonstrated their lack of acceptance by showing no knowledge of or interest in their work or subsequent success.

5 Both men enlisted the help of their closest friends to implore their parents to relinquish their immutable position. Frank Savery and Jack Beazley[1] did their best for Flecker, and Robert Phifer and Edvard Grieg[2] prevailed upon Julius Delius.

6 Financial support from the parents was cut to a minimum in the vain hope that the wayward sons would return to the fold and so follow respectable and secure careers. Flecker remained financially dependent on his parents to the end, whereas Delius eventually cast himself away from his family, both socially and financially.

7 Each man had an amanuensis to assist towards the end of his life.

8 They were both engaged in the teaching profession early in their careers. Delius was a little more successful than Flecker but they both refused to eke out their income this way.

9 Flecker and Delius left their homeland; the poet did so in order to (reluctantly) fulfill his contract with the Levant Consular Service, and

the composer because he felt his musical talents would not develop in the alien climate here. In their way they both criticised the English literary and musical circles, which, ironically, were later to give them ample recognition. Flecker expressed his feelings on this subject in a letter to his friend Mavrogordato, written in Beirut on 5 June 1912:

'. . . and what the use is of going on scratching when one can't get one's best work published I don't know.

Am in a black fury with the art of the poem . . . As for that sow the high bourgeois public it seems a poem must be crude, long and preachifying to tickle it.

Hush Marro! Don't let 'em know — but I hate *all* of them — all what you call the grey social tinges —'[4]

Goossens quotes a splendid incident concerning Delius along similar lines. The conductor was attending one of Lady Cunard's luncheon parties at the beginning of 1917, other notable guests being Thomas Beecham, Lord Balfour, Herbert Asquith, John Singer Sargent, W B Yeats, Frederick Delius, Eddie Marsh, the Duchess of Rutland, Duff Cooper and Lady Diana Manners:

'. . . Even England's two senior statesmen lapsed into silence when the Delian tones were heard asking why it was that the British public displayed such abysmal ignorance of opera as compared with other European peoples. "Don't talk like that," answered Beecham. "Just you wait till we produce *A Village Romeo and Juliet*, that'll disprove what you say." "Bah," said Delius. "The public here doesn't know a note of my music and care less!" "Perhaps," slyly observed Eddie Marsh, "that's because they don't like it." "Don't like it? Don't like it?" shouted the irate Delius. "Tell me what they *do* like!" A quiet voice interrupted with: "*Dear* Mr Balfour, *do* tell us how the Lloyd George Coalition is working," and Maud Cunard had steered the conversation into safer channels.'[5]

10   Flecker and Delius both received help from two well-known champions in their own fields. Edward Marsh did much to further Flecker's work, and Thomas Beecham was a keen advocate of Delius's music.

11   Author and composer each suffered from a degenerative disease, for which there was no known cure and from which the patients endured a lingering illness. This undoubtedly influenced Flecker's literary development and output and it has been suggested that Delius's music was similarly affected.

12   Flecker and Delius were both buried in England, but only after their devoted wives had brought their respective coffins home under unusual conditions. Flecker is buried in Cheltenham, at the foot of the Cotswolds, and Delius at Limpsfield, in beautiful Surrey countryside.

Their work

Although Flecker put into writing his desire to have real camels,[6] we do not have written evidence of his instructions for music. From the correspondence with his music master at Dean Close, Heller Nicholls, it is obvious that Flecker was sympathetic and knowledgeable about music and that he and his wife played the violin. One could conjecture that Flecker would have approved of an English composer for *Hassan* if his ideas expressed in a musical dissertation to Nicholls in March 1914 are to be relied upon:

'. . . Do you know Boosey's . . . volume of Elizabethan songs? . . . and those marvellous folksongs Cecil Sharpe has collected. I hope you are joining the pro-English musical movement and making the kids sing decent English songs instead of the vile American and German rubbish with which the Scottish Students book is stacked . . .'

However, his wife listed the musical requirements for Dean[7]:

Act I: prelude, serenade, music in the interior of Rafi's house.

Act II: prelude, ballet, chorus of beggars, poem of Ishak declaimed with music.

Act III: prelude.

Act IV: prelude, scene of Diwan, interlude between judgment scene and scene in the vaults of prison.

Act V: prelude, song of Muezzin, procession and torture scene, horror in the garden, ghosts, wind.
            Departure of the caravan chorus of pilgrims and finale.

Delius composed subtle musical accompaniments to centre with, not on, each emotional development. No musical composition could make the torture scene more palatable, and he did not try: he simply accompanied the physical sensations with musical rhythms. To take this further: when one considers the colourful themes at the heart of the play, it becomes clear that the composer's job entailed a wide embrace of sensitive, unobtrusive music which would develop with the various directions of the play and lead up to the climax of the Pilgrims but not detract from or be at variance with Flecker's unique poetry.

The composition of this 'incidental' music was no background-music commission, and by giving what he did to the score one must surely realise that some of the themes in the play touched on the nerve-centre of Delius's activity.

The composer's interest in the theatre goes back to his Paris stay (1888-90), when, as Beecham recalls, '. . . he was obsessed with the ambition to write an opera on some grand historical subject, involving the employ-ment of large resources such as processions, pageants and dancers.'[8]

The music required for *Hassan* brought him close to this love for work in the theatre and he gave to the score all the zest and energy he could muster for what was to be his last unaided musical composition.

The similarities between it and the texts of his most typical compositions are best studied by taking the key Delian themes and placing them beside those found in *Hassan* and then looking in detail at the major meeting point.

1 *The journey:* Nils, hero of his opera *Irmelin*, searches for the perfect land where he can obtain his heart's desire.

Solano, hero of another opera, *The Magic Fountain*, journeys in search of the Fountain of Eternal Youth.

Sali and Vrenchen make their final journey to peace down a river in *A Village Romeo and Juliet*.

Hassan is persuaded by Ishak to journey along 'The Golden Road to Samarkand' in search of an answer to life's vicissitudes.

2 *The fountain*: In his opera *The Magic Fountain*, Delius uses this as a symbol of Eternal Youth, as Solano explains:

'. . . Far away in the Western Isles lies the fountain of Eternal Youth. A fountain ready for those prepared to drink it in wisdom and truth.'

After a "ghostly ballet" the stage directions state that a cold green light is to flood the scene while the god of wisdom appears. Up to this point, the fountain has been a spectator but now it dictates the action. Watawa shrieks:

'. . . No, Solano! Touch not those waters. Poison lurks in that sparkling spring!' and as the fountain runs red she can only gasp:

'. . . Look, to blood it is changing. Death and destruction those waters will bring.'

In exactly the same way in *Hassan* the fountain is the central symbol to which Hassan turns when in need, and it foreshadows the action of the play. It is only when the drama has run its full course, and the fountain runs red with the blood of those innocents slaughtered, that Hassan takes 'The Golden Road to Samarkand'. Again there is a ghost scene.

3 *The quest*: The theme of searching after the unobtainable is inherent in Delius's operas. In them, the quest is after earthly love and happiness, whereas in *Hassan* the quest is on a more transcendental theme. They are searching, not so much for a God-given happiness, as an alternative life to the degradation and horrors connected with the Caliph's court. Nils, in *Irmelin*, searches for the Silver Stream, where he finds his love. Solano, in *The Magic Fountain*, searches for the Fountain of Eternal Youth. Koanga's love for Palmyra is unobtainable. Sali and Vrenchen

are thwarted lovers in *A Village Romeo and Juliet*. Niels and Fennimore embark on a tragic love-affair in *Fennimore and Gerda*.

So in *Hassan* we see Rafi and Pervaneh choosing death rather than a life of dishonour and unclean love. Hassan cannot persuade Yasmin to yield to his overtures until he becomes a respected figure in the Caliph's court, and then their love is blighted. So Ishak and Hassan search for 'a prophet who knows why men were born'.

4 *The legendary and romantic setting*: All Delius's operas fullfil this requirement, and *Hassan*, with its backcloth of the exotic east, certainly matches.

5 *The disillusionment:* All Delius's libretti, except *Irmelin*, end in disillusion. In addition, his choral works, like *Sea Drift* and the *Requiem*, and most of his songs all develop the forlorn abandonment of youth's love and ideals. The lovers in his operas settle for a suicide pact rather than live apart. Watawa and Solano die in *The Magic Fountain*; Palmyra dies with Koanga; Sali and Vrenchen choose death in *A Village Romeo and Juliet*.

In the same way, Hassan was forced to abandon his love for Yasmin and the disillusionment which set in as a result of his life in the Caliph's court set him on the Golden Road to Samarkand. Rafi allowed himself to be persuaded that death was the only solution.

6 *The unseen power*: There is a destructive, evil force to thwart the ideals of Delius's heroes. The magic fountain destroys Solano's love and life in *The Magic Fountain*; The Dark Fiddler represents the evil which destroys Sali and Vrenchen in *A Village Romeo and Juliet*; Voodoo reacts destructively for Koanga in the opera of the same name; the robbers are an unsuccessful evil force for Nils in *Irmelin*; and Fennimore is obsessed with the 'land of my dreams'.

In *Hassan*, Yasmin (with Selim) is the evil force which takes Hassan to the Caliph's company. The Caliph destroys Rafi and Pervaneh, in the same way that Hassan cannot cope with his influence.

There are many minor corresponding references in the symbolism and imagery found in their respective texts. There are repeated references to Nature: to the wind, the moon, the sun, twilight, flowers, snow, mountains, and rivers. Nature is, as it were, a backcloth, a reflection. There are references to dreamless voices, freedom, love and so on. Even their stage directions point to colours, sunrises, sunsets and other effects.

7 *Thoughts of Death and the After-life.* These are so paramount in both men's outlook and their personal views are so well reflected in their texts that the subject needs a more detailed examination.

Pagan; hedonist; heathen, atheist, pantheist; agnostic; egoist and mystic. This impressive list of labels or categories into which biographers and critics have tried to fit Delius give the reader some idea of his sentiments towards religion. He was brought up a Protestant, but according to his sister it 'had never . . . influenced him in the slightest degree.'[9] As he left home during his mid-teens, never to return, that parental influence over his spiritual development could not have been strong, and he became a very dogmatic, atheistic autocrat. Clare Delius records that for her brother:

'. . . Death was the end of everything. When the machinery of the body ceased to function, annihilation came. Nothing would make him credit that there was a hereafter . . . He made me read Nietzsche's[10] life to him, possibly hoping that this would prove a cure for what he regarded as my insanity . . . "Really, Clare, I can't imagine how an intelligent woman like you can fill your head with such nonsense".'[11]

When Eric Fenby was first rash enough to use the name 'God' in conversation with Delius he received a quick rejoinder . . . 'God? God? I don't know Him!' Another conversation concluded:

'. . . One thing is certain — that English music will never be any good till they get rid of Jesus.'[12]

Delius practised what he preached for nowhere in his work will the listener find values realised in Christian terms. There is no note of hope, no spark of optimism offered by any of his heroes, save in his first opera, *Irmelin* (1890-2). The characters either search for earthly love and happiness and this quest ends in death or disillusionment, or the characters sing of 'O past! O Happy life!' (as in *Sea Drift*).

Delius was an avid follower of Nietzsche, and even though he did not subscribe to all his teachings, he aspired to be a realist for whom there was 'only one happiness in life, and that is the happiness of creating'. His music identified itself with nature, from which source came the only renewal that Delius was to recognise.

Flecker developed his participation with organised religion further than Delius, and took greater pains to question and finally reject that part of his 'soul'. I use the word soul deliberately, for religion had entered his being and influenced his thought processes, whereas Delius never allowed religion to grip his spiritual being, and so the rejective process was not so painful. As a result of this, Delius had no fear of death, but Flecker certainly had fears and regrets.

How did his spiritual evolution take him to that frantic state of fear? At the age of 16 he wrote:

'Are we to live with never a tomorrow?
Does reason tell us deathless is our death —
Ourselves outselved, heedless of joy and sorrow,
Ever without a thought, a dream, a breath?'

He was able to find a satisfactory answer in the wonders of nature, and he concludes the poem:

'All tell us that their liveth the tomorrow,
That there *is* reawakening from our death
And mindful then as now of joy and sorrow
We shall be gods whose life is not in breath.'[13]

As he grew older he could find no easy or satisfactory answer, and he developed a fear of death because the soul would survive in a sad limbo in which it knew only that it was deprived of the joys of life on earth.

The ghost scene in *Hassan* epitomises this belief. Random extracts from his poetry centre on the same barren belief. *The Town Without a Market* is a fantasy in which the inhabitants of a graveyard lament their deprivations for 'death is darkness', and the poem ends subjectively:

'. . . Then said my heart, Death takes and cannot give.
Dark with no dream is hateful: let me live!'

Delius was very close to this in his *Requiem*, which he composed in 1914(-16):

'. . . For all who are living know that Death is coming,
but at the touch of Death lose knowledge of all things . . .'

Flecker's fear was repeated again in *No Coward's Song*. The poem begins:

'I am afraid to think about my death . . .
I know dead men are deaf . . .
I know dead men are blind . . .'

and he ends:

'O, I'd rather be
A living mouse than dead as a man dies.'

Flecker began to develop this theme at an early age. In his poem *The Shadow of a Dream*, also written when he was 16, he returns to it. Here he links it with the image of the boat or 'fairy-craft' in which the dead are unfortunate enough to travel on their journey. This reminds one of Sali and Vrenchen in Delius's opera *A Village Romeo and Juliet*, and it is a theme we find again in Flecker's poem *The Bridge of Fire*, which was published in 1907:

'. . . The wheels of time are turning, turning, turning;
The slow stream waits for thee, the stagnant mire.
   The dreamer and his dream
   Shall struggle in the stream
Sunless and unredeemable for ever,

Since this the Gods command,
That he who leaves their land
Shall travel down to that relentless river.
'O Master of the World,' I cry,
'Save me from fear of death: I dare not die.'

In the play, Hassan is found by Ishak, prostrate with horror beside the fountain after the torture scene. Hassan pleads:

'. . . Let me lie . . . This place is quiet, and the earth smells cool. May I never rise till they lift me aboard my coffin, and I'll go a sailing down the river and out to sea.'[14]

Flecker was unable to reconcile any of his guilty fears during the last few weeks of his life. On the one hand we read in a letter dictated to Hellé:

'. . . I love this world passionately and can get up neither enthusiasm for nor belief in another.'[15] And in another letter he writes: '. . . I intend to take communion this Christmas . . . But I must admit and want you to know that the general wobbliness of the English Church is a great nuisance to me and that I am bound to be as a poet a thorough ritualist and detest anything like Welsh revivals.'[16]

Frank Savery summarised Flecker's religious state on his deathbed:

'. . . his was not a mind which could settle down to the idea of revealed religion and all it entails.'[17]

He did indeed take Communion on the day he died, and among the last words he uttered was the plea: 'Lord have pity on my soul.'[18]

FOOTNOTES

[1] Jack Beazley: Sir John Beazley. A first-class classical scholar. Met Flecker at Oxford.
[2] Robert Phifer: an admirer and supporter of Delius in Danville, U.S.A. He wrote to Julius Delius and Edvard Grieg (1843-1907), met his father in London in 1889. As a result, Delius was allowed 18 months of study at Leipzig.
[3] Flecker had a little assistance from Frank Savery but most help was given by his devoted wife. Delius was also blessed with a devoted wife and many friends. He endured many more years of suffering than Flecker and was given a great deal of assistance by Eric Fenby, who went to Grez in 1928.
[4] *Some Letters From Abroad*, p65.
[5] Eugene Goossens, *Overture and Beginners* (Methuen 1951, reprinted Greenwood Press, USA, 1972), p126-7. This was an interesting confrontation between Marsh and Delius in view of their joint involvement later with *Hassan*.
[6] *Hassan*, Heinemann Drama Library series, pXV.
[7] Letter from Mme. Flecker to Basil Dean, 26 May 1920.
[8] Beecham, *op cit*, p51-2.

[9] Clare Delius, *Frederick Delius* (Nicholson and Watson, 1935), p179.
[10] Friedrich Nietzsche (1844-1900): German writer. Delius based *A Mass of Life* on his writings.
[11] *Ibid*, p180.
[12] Eric Fenby, *Delius As I Knew Him* (Icon Books, 1966) p178.
[13] Sherwood, *op cit*, p17.
[14] These important lines were omitted in the revised version of *Hassan* (Heinemann 1951).
[15] Sherwood, *op cit*, p212. Letter written late September or early October 1914.
[16] *Ibid*, p219, letter to his mother, 25 November 1914.
[17] *Ibid*, p219, Savery to Flecker's widow, 1925.
[18] *Ibid*, p221.

Chapter 5

'HASSAN' — DARMSTADT
1 JUNE 1923

Flecker had completed his five-act play by August 1913 while in the sanatorium at Leysin. When the typed copies became available later that month, Flecker sent one to Frank Savery on 28 August. Savery was in Munich at the time, and Flecker asked his friend to 'tell me the crude truth about it'. While Savery was reading it, Ernst Freissler also read and admired the play so much that he bought the German translation rights. Of this development Flecker commented to Savery on 1 September 1913:

> '. . . *Certainly* show it to your friend. Certainly let it be translated if there's any chance of it being *played*. But it can't be published till after it's played in England — if it ever is. Try and get it taken by a German theatre by all means. Only I know you will only show it to honourable men and friends of yours.'[1]

He ended the letter with a caution about literary pirates.

Flecker revealed the financial side of this transaction in a letter to his mother in October 1913:

> '. . . I have sold my rights for the German translation of my play, *Hassan*, for £15, and £5 for subsequent editions. The publisher becomes also my agent for the stage . . . the famous firm of Langen.'[2]

The history of the play in Germany between August 1913 and June 1923 is recorded in a letter from Albert Langen to Messrs A P Watt and Son, written on 26 August 1921:

> '. . . The German translation of "Hassan" of Mr James Elroy Flecker, whose death meanwhile I have learnt with sincere regret, was made by Mr Freissler in the Spring of 1914 and was at once put in the Press by us. The piece had just been printed, and printed stage copies had been sent to the German theatres when, at the beginning of August 1914, the war broke out. It will be straightway clear to you that during the war a play by a living English author would have no prospect of being produced in Germany. Under these circumstances we kept back the issue of the book until the end of the war and published it in 1919 and once more renewed our endeavours to get the piece performed on German stages. Immediately after the end of the war we wrote to Mr Flecker in Montana sur Sierre, but our letter was returned to us, marked "unknown" and we did not know where to address ourselves in order to get at Mr Flecker, who had no doubt meantime, died. The fee for the first impression of the book edition of "Hassan" was received by Mr Flecker, to the amount of £15, in 1913, immediately after signature of the contract. The eight paper covered and four bound free copies agreed under the contract are being sent to you by this post, to be handed

to Mrs Flecker. There were great difficulties in the way of the stage performance of the piece. On the one hand, even after the conclusion of peace, theatres hesitated to perform pieces by living English authors, unless they were known, like Bernard Shaw, and on the other hand, the beautiful piece of Mr Flecker, as you are no doubt aware, involves great difficulties of staging. At last, after long efforts we succeeded in finding a theatre which has acquired the piece for first performance in Germany. We are glad to be able to inform you and Mrs Flecker that this is the Darmstädter hessische Landestheater (Darmstadt Hessian Provincial Theatre) which is under the management of a new and very active Director, Mr Hartung and is reckoned among the best and as one of the leading theatres of Germany. We hope that Hartung will produce the piece in a manner which will be calculated to result in great success and open up the way for its appearance in other German theatres. Hartung has also acquired the first right of performance of the piece and proposes to make this first performance in January 1922. We are informing Hartung of your address and we think that he will apply to you in order to get the music of Frederick Delius which, as we hear, was composed by the latter for "Hassan".'

The German translation was made from the unamended Leysin Version, apart from a couple of minor alterations. On page 17 the King of the Beggars loses the line 'When high office is polluted . . .' to Hassan, and on page 33 the Hauptmann and the Führer exchange a speech. These minor alterations could be put down to printing errors.

Flecker explained the work on his amendments in a note to Savery on 2 June 1914 in which he said he was:

'. . . revising, considerably shortening, and vastly improving *Hassan*. Whatever Dean does to it afterward, this is *my* version for publication and the German stage.'

He continued with a hopeful question:

'Will you therefore get Freissler to send me his copy of the MS. so that I can write in the alterations. There is very little added so that I hope it won't give Freissler much extra work.'

By this time, however, Freissler had completed the translation with the aid of Herbert Alberti and so the improvements were not included. Flecker wrote to Savery on 11 June to acknowledge his letter and MS.:

'. . . I don't mind a bit *Hassan* appearing in its old version in German and shan't ask Freissler to make any changes.'

But on 26 June, Flecker had changed his mind and wrote another hopeful letter to Savery:

'. . . if Freissler is keen he might alter the end of Act IV in accordance with the new text and add Pervaneh's new speeches in the Ghost Scene. The other alterations in IV and V are unimportant or else interdependent. His proofs wouldn't be hurt by these.'

These alterations were not included, and Hellé renewed the poet's wish in 1922, as she later explained in a letter to Heller Nicholls:[4]

James Elroy Flecker

Hassan

Die Geschichte des Hassan von Bagdad
und wie er dazu kam
den goldenen Weg nach Samarkand
zu ziehen

Ein Schauspiel in fünf Akten

Deutsch von Ernst W. Freißler
und Herbert Alberti

Albert Langen, München

The title-page of 'Hassan' as published in Germany (Langen).

41

'. . . The translation has unfortunately been done on an older unrevised text. I last year asked the translator to revise it at least for the stage. I doubt whether he has done so. It is a great nuisance the play should be first given in translation but I can't prevent this.'[3]

It is worth observing that the songs in Freissler and Alberti's version generally failed to follow the metre of their originals, and were therefore useless in conjunction with Delius's music. The publishers of the latter, Universal Edition, therefore commissioned new translations from R. St. Hoffmann, and these appear in the vocal scores.

Although January 1922 was given as the proposed date for this production, it was delayed for 17 months. In December 1922 Jelka Delius wrote to Granville Bantock[5] from Frankfurt-am-Main:

'. . . In February Elroy Flecker's drama "Hassan" to which Delius has written *Musique de Scène* will be produced at Darmstadt near here . . . We shall be here for 2 or 3 months still.'

However, on 15 February 1923, Heller Nicholls wrote to Mme. Flecker, acknowledging receipt of one of the German translations and saying:

'. . . Yesterday I had a letter from Mrs Delius saying she will let me know the exact date. I do hope it will be in April . . .'

Jelka did write to Heller Nicholls from Bad Oyenhausen on 2 May — not to give him the date of the production, though, but to tell Nicholls of their plans:

'. . . [we are] staying here for my husband to take the baths . . . I really do not know when *Hassan* will be done at Darmstadt. They said in May, but we got tired of waiting for it, especially as it will be brought out in London in the autumn . . . we shall stay here till end of May and then go to Norway.'

But it was not until 1 June 1923 that the play was finally produced. Delius did not attend the performances, despite the fact that he was staying at Bad Oyenhausen, about 22 miles from Darmstadt. He was in 'bad health' then, as Dean had witnessed when he visited him there at the beginning of May in order that he could clear up 'all points as to how he wants the music played, and so forth', as he described in a letter to Mme. Flecker on 11 May.

Either the theatre had not informed the Deliuses or Madame Flecker of their proposed date, or the play was mounted in a terrific rush, for by mid-May no-one had been informed of the production date, and Hellé later recounted the haste with which she endeavoured to reach Darmstadt after the news of the production had been sent to her at the end of May. In the same letter to Heller Nicholls on 30 May she confessed she knew not a word of German '(except titles of Schumann songs — not much use for travelling purposes).' However, Herr Hartung's secretary knew a few words and Hellé

42

felt more at home. But she expressed disappointment at the lack of English support:

> '. . . I do wish some of Roy's literary friends could have been here but Jack Squire is "tied to his desk" as he told me and as for Jack Beazley, there is no possibility of moving *him*. I can't understand the absence of Mr and Mrs Delius. I thought they would be sure to be there.'

I can do no better than describe the performance as witnessed by the two key figures, Mme. Flecker and Dean. She was the first to see it and described her visit in a letter to Dean on 5 June:

> '. . . I have just returned from Darmstadt. *Hassan* was performed there on Friday and was a very great success in spite of the present state of mind of the Germans.
>
> Herr Hartung (the producer) had unfortunately to leave out the ghost scene and I think the last part was hurried and greatly spoilt by the last scene being also suppressed and reduced to a far away tinkling of camel-bells and a voice *singing* the poem in the distance. At the last moment the scene of the two beggars by the fountain had to be cut, scene II beginning by the rescued Caliph saying "Is my palace safe?" The scene ending Act I was not shortened (Ishak's monologue) I believe it could be. The great scene between Hassan and Yasmin was wonderful, both actors were remarkable, in fact I believe I shall never see a truer Hassan than this Falk[sic]. The great scene between Rafi and Pervaneh though it shook the public was much too howled from beginning to end. The ballet was too heavy and I believe the *singing* is a mistake. The setting was admirable all through in the best Persian miniature style. The actors move very little and the general stillness enhances the effect of the spoken words. The diction and voices were excellent: on the whole a most remarkable performance. I'm sorry you could not come. It will probably be given again late in September (the theatre closes this month and opens again in September). I'll send you some of the press-cuttings which have been promised me. Owing to the difficulties of travel presently existing in Germany I don't believe there was a single Englishman in or about Darmstadt so that nothing much will be heard in England. I don't know German and it was rather like a nightmare for me this first production in German.
>
> Anyway what one can learn from this production is that the play must go quicker at the beginning and slower at the end — in other words that the cuttings must be made chiefly in the first three acts, that the ghost-scene ought to be kept and made as short as possible while the procession of protracted death must not be hurried. The scene between Yasmin and Masrur is very effective. The caravan must be seen leaving and the poem must be recited and not sung, also the singing in the ballet is no good. I am sorry Delius wrote those songs, they seem to me useless. I would not have either the man who sings behind the scene while Hassan recites the serenade.'

Basil Dean *was* able to go to Darmstadt and see the final performance of that season on 16 June (the run was not continuous), and it is clear that he did not agree with some of Mme. Flecker's opinions:

> '. . . The performance was a great disappointment. I find myself in warm agreement with you about Delius's music in many respects. The fault is not entirely his. A great deal of it is due to the way it was handled. I am sending you a copy of my letter to Delius . . .
>
> Frankly I cannot agree with you as to the Hassan. I thought he was full of stage tricks, and I shall be bitterly disappointed if we do not do better in England. In fact, I

thought the whole rendering of the play nothing more than a very good provincial attempt under severe financial and other handicaps.'

In his letter to Delius,[6] Dean wrote:

'. . . I thought the music indifferently rendered. It did not seem to me that the audience were made sufficiently aware of the music, nor did it appear that the music had been so handled as to aid the atmosphere. Neither the poet's nor the musician's point of view was realised, and as to a union between the two elements, that had not been thought of.'

Mme. Flecker replied in personal tones:

'. . . I am glad you wrote to Delius about those songs. I quite understand you should have been disappointed with the production. I feared much worse and besides I was so upset by the whole thing that I am afraid my critical faculties were rather numbed.'

She continued to relate to Mr Nicholls her impressions of her visit to Darmstadt and the German production, on 22 June:

'. . . The performance was remarkable in some respects but the end of the play was completely spoilt by the suppression of the last Caravan scene, and the ballet and singing were frankly bad. I thought Delius' music interesting in some parts but badly rendered. The reception by the public was most enthusiastic on the first night, in spite of the very unfavourable moment chosen by Hartung for the production of a foreign play. Violent attacks had been made against him on this subject and the German 'fascists' have threatened to kill him. The press was on the whole very offensive as was to be expected.'

Between June and September of that year, Dean was working hard to ensure a superior production of the play. He realised he had not requested sufficient music in 1920 and he now had to extract these additions 'from a loudly protesting composer'.[7] It is not surprising that Delius complained. The fact that he was ill, having suffered 'a sort of physical-nervous breakdown',[8] meant he could not write at all.

Dean's letter of requests, dated 19 June, would have arrived either on 21 June, the day Delius left for his cottage in Norway, or possibly even later. It therefore reached not only a sick composer, but also one who had a strenuous journey from which to recover. Jelka assisted as much as she could with the work and Delius received a timely visit from Percy Grainger.[9]

FOOTNOTES

[1] *Some Letters From Abroad of James Elroy Flecker, op cit,* p106.

[2] Hodgson, *op cit.* p191.

[3] 8 February 1923.

[4] Heller (William Henry) Nicholls; music-master at Dean Close School, who took a keen interest in Flecker's career.

[5] Granville Bantock (1868-1946): English composer and conductor, later professor at Birmingham University.

[6] For the first time we know that it was this letter from Dean to Delius 19 June 1923 that gave rise to all the alterations and additions listed in *A Catalogue of the Music Archive of the Delius Trust, London* by Rachel Lowe (Boosey and Hawkes, 1974).

[7] Dean, *op cit,* p146.

[8] Letter from Jelka Delius to Bantock, 27 December 1922.

[9] Percy Grainger (1882-1961): Australian-born composer and pianist who became a close friend of Delius. His contribution to the score of *Hassan* is detailed in Chapter 7.

ILLUSTRATIONS

Acknowledgments

BASIL DEAN — pages from the programme of the original production at His Majesty's Theatre 1923; also the postcard illustration of the theatre.

DELIUS TRUST — photograph of Frederick Delius, Jelka Delius and Percy Grainger.

DELIUS TRUST and BOOSEY and HAWKES — page 43 of the musical score (the former own the manuscript, the latter the copyright).

DR OSWALD BILL — illustration from Act III, Scene 2, Darmstadt.

BODLEIAN LIBRARY, OXFORD — pages from the manuscript of the Leysin version.

James Elroy Flecker, Beirut 1912.

Jelka Delius, Percy Grainger and (seated) Frederick Delius, in Frankfurt, March 1923.

Page 43 from the manuscript of Delius's original score for 'Hassan'. The music is part of the 'Divertissement'. In the original MS the composer's shaky pencil can be detected beneath the inking-in of another hand. The names of the instruments are in the hand of Jelka Delius.

49

Yasmin (Cathleen Nesbitt) and Selim (Esmé Percy) mock Hassan in Act I, Scene II of the London production (from 'The Sketch', October 10, 1923).

The Calif (Malcolm Keen) presiding in Act III, Scene III (played as Scene II) of the London production (from 'The Sketch', November 7, 1923).

who ever saw a confectioner like this!
Where did you learn poetry Hassan
of my heart?

Hassan: In that great school the market
of Bagdad. For thee (master of the world) poetry is a princely
diversion; but
for us it was a deliverance from hell.

Page 5 of Act III, Scene I of the Leysin version, showing Flecker's pencil am.

> heaven/
your eyes to ~~the stars~~/to hear the tune.

HASSAN   No mystery, Master, ~~attended thy servant's birth. My~~
~~father was a confectioner, and his father too. If~~
~~thou doubtest, look at me. Alas, have I the stature,~~
~~the grace,~~ the outline of nobility?

CALIPH   But ~~whence~~ your poetry - and whence your carpets?
~~Have you had a great Teacher?~~

HASSAN   Master, I have not ~~sat~~ at the feet of the wise nor
~~sucked honey from the lips of philosophers.~~ But as
~~for Poetry,~~ I have learnt to read and I have loved to
hear. Poetry is the delight of Princes, but it is
~~the deliverance of the poor.~~ ~~For~~ Allah made poetry
a cheap thing ~~for a man~~ to buy and a simple thing ~~for~~
~~a man~~ to understand. He gave men dreams by night that
they might learn to dream by day. ~~It is above all~~
~~poor~~ men who work ~~very~~ hard ~~who~~ have need of these
dreams. All the town of Bagdad is passionate for
poetry, O master. Dost thou not know what great crowds
gather to hear the epic of Antari sung in the streets
at evening? I have seen ~~the~~ cobblers weep and ~~the~~
butchers bury their great faces in their hands!

CALIPH   By Eblis and the powers of Hell, should I not know
this, and know that therein lies the secret of the

s blue crayon marks the long cuts; his wife's alterations are written in ink.

Act IV, Scene 2, in the London production: the lovers – Rafi (Basil Gill) and Pervaneh (Laura Cowie) – choosing their fate.

Act V, Scene 1: Yasmin (Cathleen Nesbitt) eagerly awaits the Procession of Protracted Death which Hassan (Henry Ainley) is forced to witness.

The final scene in the London production, with Henry Ainley (left) as Hassan and Leon Quartermaine as Ishak.

Act III, Scene 2 in the London production: Hassan (Henry Ainley) attempts to kill Yasmin (Cathleen Nesbitt). Below: the same scene in the Darmstadt production (Herr Valk and Fräulein Lisso).

*

The Hessische Landes-Theater at Darmstadt (above) and His Majesty's Theatre in London.

*

Chapter 6

'HASSAN' — LONDON
20 SEPTEMBER 1923

Although Delius had written much of the music for the play by the end of 1920, just over two years elapsed before Dean was able to see a solution to the major problem which beset his plans for *Hassan*, namely, finding a theatre large enough to stage his lavish production. The breakthrough came in a most unexpected way. Dean was in hospital early in 1923 when Messrs Grossmith and Malone[1] came to see him:

'. . . Grossmith, after much courteous enquiry, proceeded with much charm and circumlocution to broach the purpose of their visit. *East of Suez* was still doing well, but plans for the future had to be made . . . "Would I direct a revival of Arthur Pinero's *The Gay Lord Quex* with himself as the gay lord?" In an inspired moment, induced possibly by a rising temperature, I thought, "Here is the opening for *Hassan* at last!" After an appropriate show of diffidence I said: "Yes, I will do it for you if you will let me do *Hassan* immediately afterwards." In such prosaic language was our bargain struck and the way to fulfilment of my promise made clear . . .'[2]

Hassan became a reality at last! Dean was determined to match the quality of Flecker's words and the beautiful music with a lavish production, and so with hopes of a greatly superior production and a longer run than Darmstadt he began to fulfil the promise made to Flecker nine years previously. Moreover, as he and his musical friends considered the piano score to be of the highest quality, both in itself and for the play, he 'determined upon similar distinction in all branches of the production'.[3]

Before going on to describe the production I want to go through the evolution of this musical score. As related in Chapter 3, Dean had chosen Delius after being enthralled with the well-known entr'acte music, *The Walk to the Paradise Garden*, from his opera *A Village Romeo and Juliet*.

The first major musical problem to be overcome was not the short time allowed to the composer (for Delius was willing to set to work immediately) but the size of orchestra Dean could afford to engage. The subject was raised by Mme. Flecker in her letter of 27 July 1920 to Dean:

'. . . [Delius] seems rather worried about the extremely reduced numbers of the orchestra you can afford him. Would it not be possible, the theatre being so small, to take a little space from *under* the stage in which a row of instruments might be added? . . . If you could have thirty instruments it would be so much better. No modern composer could I am afraid manage with less . . .'

At this stage in the discussions, the larger stage of His Majesty's Theatre had not been suggested. However, it was not space that made Dean adamant over the size of orchestra; it was his budget. He replied to Mme. Flecker two days later:

'. . . I think it will be quite impossible to have an orchestra of 30 musicians for "HASSAN" . . . An orchestra of 30 musicians would cost something like £200 per week and "HASSAN" is, as you know, a very big production and requires a good many people besides a big stage staff. It would therefore be very unwise to spend too much on the music. We should only have to cut down some other department. I have promised Mr Delius 21 musicians . . . I am prepared to allow one or two more over the 21, but certainly not more than that. The trouble of course is that Mr Delius is accustomed more to Operatic work where an orchestra of 60 is nothing.'

It appears that they came to a working agreement over this problem, at least for the time being, and Delius used 26 players. However, he did not let the matter rest there, for at the two rehearsals Delius attended Eugene Goossens[4] recalled that:

'. . . [he] had been peevish at rehearsals, especially about tempi and dynamics . . . "The Golden Road to Samarkand," though atmospheric and wistful, was not enhanced by the Merchants of Bagdad singing off pitch, back stage . . . This infuriated Delius: he shouted, "We must have a larger orchestra; they can't hear the orchestra." To which Basil answered, "You can't have a larger orchestra, Mr Delius. This production is costing enough as it is."'[5]

For all Delius's complaining about the limited numbers afforded him, he composed the music quickly, for Dean recalled that:

'. . . the greatest part of the music was delivered with what I regarded as unwelcome speed, since I was still without concrete plans for the production.'[6]

The official agreement was not signed by Dean and Delius until 23 November 1920, and then only after much haggling. Dean's manager, E P Clift, found the composer a difficult person to negotiate with, as Dean related:

'. . . When I received news in America the following Autumn [1920] that he had totally rejected the draft agreement my manager had drawn up, and was demanding that Philip Heseltine[7] should be placed in charge of all musical arrangements, my impression that he was unlikely to be flustered in a business argument was confirmed. Further drafts of the agreement were submitted, amended and returned, so that my manager, completely nonplussed by his first encounter with a famous composer, wrote to me in America that "this is the most difficult gentleman I ever had to deal with".'[8]

One letter chosen from the many between Delius and Heseltine illustrates their close working alliance. On 29 August 1920, Delius wrote:

'. . . I received Dean's letter accepting my conditions the day after you left. Enclosed I send you a letter I received from him this morning concerning the conducting.
I think we shall get it in the end all the same, namely, in this way: I am writing to

Dean today and am suggesting that you shall attend all the rehearsals, that you conduct the chorus behind the scenes free of charge and that you conduct the performances when the other man has a day off or is any way prevented. In this we shall gradually get there.'

As mentioned in Chapter 5, Dean requested several alterations and additions to the score after he had seen the Darmstadt production. Jelka described how she helped her husband in a letter to Marie Clews[9] on 4 August 1923:

'. . . I have had to help Fred composing as he cannot write the small notes which he dictates to me. Then I had to copy the whole orchestral score here, 52 big pages. These were additions to the music and they were waiting impatiently for them in London.'

Heseltine refers to Jelka's assistance in his review of the play which was published in *The Daily Telegraph* on 29 September 1923:

'. . . All these additional numbers . . . have been composed and scored by dictation to Mrs Delius, the composer having been unable during his recent illness to hold a pen.'

The additions (and alterations) Jelka refers to were requested by Dean after he had seen the German production. In a letter to the composer, dated 19 June 1923, he discussed some of them:

'. . . There are one or two points which I feel I should bring to your notice at once. One is that the treatment of Hassan's poem underneath Yasmin's window is not a success. It is simply distracting because at one moment one is endeavouring to listen to the words of the poem, and the other to catch the tones of the song. I fear we shall have to resign ourselves to the fact that this is just one of those many experiments in the theatre that on this occasion does not come off. I will of course try it at rehearsal here, but I am pretty sure I am right.'

It was originally scored for Hassan to recite the poem while a wordless tenor voice was accompanied by a piano behind the scene, the harp playing between the vocal phrases. Dean goes on to suggest that '. . . we shall have to use a harp or some instrument that you select, in the orchestra, and leave the actor to speak the poem with a faint musical undercurrent.'[10]

In the play as performed in London, the orchestra played while Hassan rendered the lines, and the tenor only sang the melody as an interlude later.

Dean's second request to Delius was in respect of the Scene of the Moving Walls:

'. . . the singing and ballet in the scene was most muddled' —

[Mme. Flecker had dismissed this part as 'no good'.]

'and I see that my first view about this thing is correct. We shall have to treat it quite frankly as "A Song and Dance Scena" as the old-fashioned play books used to describe it. The ballet movement will have to begin at the very start of the singing, the ballet will have to be lengthened out and worked up into a climax at the end of the "Divertissement." Thirdly, the Soldiers' Song at the beginning of the Divan does not work up into a climax as rendered. You will recall that I pointed this out to you, and you explained that this was merely a question of the orchestration and that it could be altered in rehearsal. There is an alteration in the Tempo in the middle of the song which, from my point of view, is dangerous. The song instead of being treated as a ballad should be sung with terrific vigour, and the soldiers will come sweeping down a broad flight of circular steps on to an otherwise empty stage as they sing . . .'

Dean, of course, had been attending to other aspects of the production and one formidable obstacle was the censor. The stage of 1923 was tightly governed by him and Dean was told that the torture scene would prevent him from being granted the license. However, he persuaded Lord Cromer (who currently held the office) to read the play with the understanding that the scene in question would not be realistically represented on stage, and in this way the licence was obtained. Fortunately Flecker had foreseen part of that problem before he sent the Leysin version to the typist. He went through the text substituting a sword for the whip and cutting some of the dialogue in Act III Scene 2. He told Savery:

'. . . Hassan originally was going to try and whip Yasmin, not to kill her. But I decided that it would be too sadistic and not serious enough.'[12]

This theme had long been a part of Flecker's private life. During Christmas 1911 T. E. Lawrence[13] visited the Fleckers in Beirut and the two men (who shared a common interest in poetry) had a conversation, with Flecker 'carelessly flung beneath a tree, talking of women's slippers and of whippings, of revising *Hassan*'.[14] John Sherwood discusses this aspect of his life in his biography of the poet.

Once Dean had gained permission to stage the play, and the production date had been firmly fixed, he could give all his assistants the go-ahead to work at their various tasks. George Harris had begun the work of designing the sets, scenery and costumes as early as June 1920 (partly because Dean did hope to produce it earlier and partly to appease Mme. Flecker). To a certain extent he had to keep to the style which Mme. Flecker tactfully reminded Dean on 9 June 1920 that

'. . . my husband would have liked them to be — "not vaguely oriental but strictly Persian" as he writes in the Scenario. I am sending you, under separate cover, some of the illustrations of the "Arabian Nights" which he had in view and I would ask you to give them to your designer who could simply copy some of the costumes and get ideas for the scenery, these illustrations being reproductions of real Persian manuscript miniatures.'

On the title page of the Leysin Version, Flecker had written by hand the following instructions:
(The scenery and costumes of this play are to be strictly Persian, not vaguely oriental. They should be inspired by the Persian Miniatures of which the

Illustrations to Mardrus' big edition of the Arabian Nights form an admirable collection. The miniatures are of course 500 years later than the actual Haroun al Rashid epoch; but it is not the historical but legendary monarch who is here presented. The Mongol element in the pictures must however be avoided by the designer of costumes.)

Dean replied in pacifying tones on 11 June:

> '. . . I think you need have no fear as to the method of production in respect of scenery and costumes. You may or may not know that the designer who does all the work for my Company is already looked upon as one of the big designers for the English stage. He is also a cultured man who would not do anything which would in any way rival "CHU CHIN CHOW"! I shall, however, welcome your illustrations of the "ARABIAN NIGHTS".'

A week later he could write to say:

> '. . . You will be delighted to hear that the design for the Street of Felicity has just been completed . . . and I think it is magnificent, quite one of the best of his that I have ever seen. I make no doubt whatever that you will be delighted with the scene when you see it and I only hope that the other scenes will come as readily to his imagination. He is very grateful to you for the Persian reproductions you sent, and tells me they will be very useful to him and that they are quite in accord with his own conceptions of what are wanted.'

The design for the famous basket scene in The Street of Felicity involved a mechanical engineer to advise the stage director to ensure the safe delivery of the basket each time.

Dean was gaining a name for himself on account of his very clever and imaginative lighting effects, and one in particular is worth explaining. For the dawn light at the beginning of Act I Scene 2 and Act II Scene 2, Dean achieved an effective prismatic light by fixing extension pieces to the fronts of a dozen projectors so that the broken lenses (which happened frequently, due to poor ventilation) could be set at an angle of 45 degrees to the lamps. These were aimed on the white street walls which had been coated with a mixture of whitening and ground mica, and the final prismatic effect was to make the audience gasp with approval.

All this designing and planning went on throughout 1920 and continued well into the next year, but as yet no firm date for the production had been fixed. Alongside the design work, Dean was giving serious consideration to the choice of actors. Both Dean and Mme. Flecker agreed as early as June 1920 that Mr Moscovitch would be admirable as Hassan and that Cathleen Nesbitt would play Pervaneh well. Nothing came of their first suggestion and Cathleen Nesbitt's name was superseded by Gilda Varesa, a suggestion Marsh was 'quite thrilled' about. In fact, Cathleen Nesbitt played Yasmin in the production and Laura Cowie was Pervaneh, both actresses doing 'their best with parts for which neither of them was temperamentally suited'.[15] Isabel Jeans and Fay Compton later took over the rôle of Yasmin. Henry

Thursday, September 20th, 1923, at 7.30 p.m.
Subsequently at 8 p.m.

GEORGE GROSSMITH and J. A. E. MALONE'S PRODUCTION

OF

"HASSAN"

and how he came to make the Golden Journey to Samarkand

A Play in Five Acts

by

JAMES ELROY FLECKER

Arranged for Production on the Stage by BASIL DEAN

The Characters in the Order of their Appearance :

HASSAN, a Confectioner	by Mr. Henry Ainley
SELIM..	,, Mr. S. Esmé Percy *
YASMIN	,, Miss Cathleen Nesbitt
A PORTER	,, Mr. Sydney Bland
THE CALIPH, Haroun Al Raschid ..	,, Mr. Malcolm Keen *
ISHAK, his Minstrel..	,, Mr. Leon Quartermaine
JAFAR, his Vizier	,, Mr. Frank Cochrane
MASRUR, his Executioner	,, Mr. Edmund Willard
RAFI, King of the Beggars	,, Mr. Basil Gill
ALDER	,, Miss Rita Page
WILLOW } slaves	,, Miss Kitty McCoy
JUNIPER	,, Miss Maureen Dillon
TAMARISK	,, Miss Eileen Raven
BEGGAR }	,, Mr. Nicholas Nadegin
LEADERS	,, Mr. Robert East
ALI } nondescripts	,, Mr. Ivor Barnard *
ABDU	,, Mr. Andrew Leigh
THE CHIEF OF THE POLICE	,, Mr. Alfred Clark
THE CAPTAIN OF THE MILITARY ..	,, Mr. Tarver Penna
A HERALD	,, Mr. Douglas Burbidge
PERVANEH	,, Miss Laura Cowie

* These Artistes appear by permission of REANDEAN

Cast-list pages from the programme of the 1923 London production.

Characters at the Caliph's Court :

THE PRINCE OF BASRA..	..	.. .. by Mr. Frank Vosper
THE PRINCE OF DAMASCUS ..	..	.. „ Mr. Claude Delaval
THE PRINCE OF KONIAH	..	' .. „ Mr. Osborn Adair
THE GOVERNOR OF KHORASAN	..	.. „ Mr. Harrison Lawson
A CALIGRAPHIST ..	.. ..	.. „ Mr. Thomas Waters
A WRESTLER	.. ..	.. .. „ Mr. B. E. Evremonde
ABU NOWAS, the Caliph's Jester	..	.. „ Mr. Sidney Bland
THE RAJAH OF THE UPPER GANGES	..	„ Mr. C. R. Stone
THE CHINESE PHILOSOPHER	..	.. „ Mr. Ivor Barnard
A DERVISH ..	.. .. ..	.. „ Mr. Caton-Woodville
THE AMBASSADOR OF THE EMPRESS IRENE		„ Mr. Vivian Carew

Characters in the Last Poem :

HASSAN	.. ..	.. .. by Mr. Henry Ainley
ISHAK ..	.. .. ..	.. .. „ Mr. Leon Quartermaine
THE MASTER OF THE CARAVAN ..	..	.. „ Mr. S. Esmé Percy
THE CHIEF DRAPER	.. ..	.. .. „ Mr. Frank Vosper
THE CHIEF GROCER	.. ..	.. .. „ Mr. Douglas Burbidge
THE PRINCIPAL JEW	.. ..	.. .. „ Mr. Tarver Penna
THE WATCHMAN..	.. ..	.. .. „ Mr. Frank Cochrane
A WOMAN ..	.. .. ..	.. .. „ Miss Dartrey
AN OLD MAN	.. .. ..	.. .. „ Mr. Charles R. Stone

Soldiers, Police, Dancing Women, Beggars, Mutes, Attendants, Merchants, Camel Drivers, Jews, Pilgrims, Torturers, Casual Loiterers :
by
Messrs. Talbot Homewood, R. D. Whitaker, Eric Fowler, James Lomas, G. Dunstall, Laurence Attridge, Roy Leaker, Roy Rich, G. Bailey
Mesdames Evelyn Taylor, Fabia Drake

Choristers :

Messrs. M. Marianni, W. Rogers, A. D. Gollan, Harold Farrar, R. Gibson, Arthur Mortimer, A. J. Willard, Edgar Pierce, E. Hughes, David Hodder, C. Cornock, P. Wilson, E. Ward, Edwin Negus, Selwyn Morgan, Hugh McNeill
Mesdames Adine Barrett, Violet Patterson, Laura Vivian, Loti Ford, Vivian Jefferies, Jean Imray, Betty Hayman, Katherine Coleridge, Violet Beaumont, Vivian Lambelet, Fay Yeatman, Kathleen Beldon, Constance Taylor, Linda Harris, Nellie Griffiths, Millicent Cane

Male Ballet :

Messrs. George Wolkowsky, Jack Triesalt, Jack Renshaw, L. Lucas, W. Scott, Aubrey Hitchins, Leon Kelloway, Alex. Artirov, Keith Lester, Caird Leslie

Female Ballet :

Mesdames Ann Tewksbury, Peggy Mackenzie, Ursula Moreton, B. Ostrehan, Dyta Morena, Audrey Carlyon, Rosalind Wade, Vera Temple, Margot St. Ledger, Renée Gadd, Vivienne Bennett, Hélène Saxova, Joane Wolfe, Eliane Ferrars, Babette Moore

The Music composed by Frederick Delius
The Scenery and Costumes designed by George W. Harris
The Ballets arranged by Michel Fokine
The whole Production planned and rehearsed by Basil Dean

Ainley played Hassan superbly well for he had 'an infallible ear for the music of words', and Leon Quartermaine played Ishak.

Dean engaged Michel Fokine to arrange the ballets. He explained that Fokine 'was the original of the Russian Ballet Choreographers and by far the soundest of the lot.' He goes on to record their meeting and how it came about. Dean was in America in 1922 but not enjoying his successes as much as he might because anxiety about *Hassan* was increasing rather than diminishing. Both Mme. Flecker and Delius were growing restive under the long delay. To make matters worse, Alec Rea had dug his toes in: there were to be no more advance payments to the poet's widow.

But notwithstanding, Dean persuaded a manager-producer friend, Charles B. Dillingham, to introduce him to Fokine:

> '. . . Over a sumptuous dinner Charlie told the great *maître de ballet* fabulous tales about the play, which he had not read, and about the wonderful ballet music, which he had not heard. I think Fokine was more impressed by the composer's name than by Charlie's ebullience. I was overjoyed when he agreed, subject to reservations as to date, to come to London to compose the ballets. This information helped me to restrain Mme. Flecker from bolting with the script of the play in her teeth, so to speak, into the arms of another producer.'[16]

Many dancers were auditioned, from Scotland to Paris, first by Roger Ould and then by Willie Warde,[17] and from their preliminary choice Fokine chose his 25.

Mme. Flecker was very keen to have the play published and as early as December 1919 she told Dean that she would instruct the literary advisors to contact a publisher. Dean, however, was not at all enthusiastic to encourage publication of a play that was about to appear on the stage as 'plays that are published beforehand remain stillborn nine times out of ten.'[18] Two years later Mme. Flecker insisted on its publication and it appeared in September 1922; happily it was a publication which proved the exception to Dean's rule. This version was presented in five acts, and was reprinted 23 times. Dean's revised, three-act version was printed in 1951 and again has been reprinted several times.

STRUCTURE OF THE TWO PUBLISHED VERSIONS

1922			1951	
Act I	Scene 1		Act I	Scene 1
	2			2
Act II	Scene 1			3
	2			4
Act III	Scene 1	played together	Act II	Scene 1
	2	in London 1923		
	3			2
Act IV	Scene 1	not performed in London 1923	Act III	Scene 1
	2			2
Act V	Scene 1			3
	2			4

ACT I.

SCENE 1.—*A Room behind the Shop of Hassan the Confectioner, in old Bagdad.*

Three Minutes Interval.

SCENE 2.—*The Street of Felicity by the Fountain of the Two Pigeons. Moonlight. The Same Day.*

Three Minutes Interval.

ACT II.

SCENE 1.—*A Room in the House of the Moving Walls. The Same Night.*

Three Minutes Interval.

SCENE 2.—*In the Street of Felicity again. Dawn of the Day following.*

Eight Minutes Interval.

ACT III.

SCENE 1.—*A Private Apartment within a Pavilion in the Garden of the Caliph. The Same Day.*

Three Minutes Interval.

SCENE 2.—*The Outer Hall of the Palace. The Caliph's Divan on the Afternoon of the Same Day.*

Eight Minutes Interval.

ACT IV.

SCENE 1.—*In the Vaults of the Palace. Towards Sunset of the Same Day.* (N.B.—*This Scene will not be performed*).

SCENE 2.—*The Cell of the King of the Beggars. At Sunset.*

Three Minutes Interval.

ACT V.

SCENE 1.—*The Garden of the Palace of the Caliph in Front of the Pavilion. Nightfall of the following Day.*

Four Minutes Interval.

SCENE 2.—*At the Gate of the Moon, Bagdad. Towards Dawn of the Morrow.*

For the comfort and convenience of the audience it is suggested that they remain seated during all but the two long intervals

---

The Special Orchestra conducted at the First Performance by Eugene Goossens.

The Scenery made by Brunskill, London ; and Robinson, Liverpool ; and painted by Cecil J. Cross, and Alec. Johnstone.

The Costumes made by Simmons, and Grossmith and Malone Wardrobe. The Wigs by Clarkson. The Shoes by Rayne.

The Lighting by the Producer from Special Material supplied by Schwabe & Co., Berlin, T. J. Digby, and General Electric Co., London.

Stage Manager	*William Abingdon.*	
Assistant Stage Managers	*David Franklin & Sydney Bland.*	
Musical Director	*Percy Fletcher.*	
Manager	*Carl. F. Leyel.*	

Extracts from the Rules made by the Lord Chamberlain.—1.—The name of the actual and responsible Manager of the Theatre must be printed on every playbill. 2.—The Public can leave the Theatre at the end of the performance by all exit and entrance doors, which must open outwards. 3.—Where there is a fireproof screen to the proscenium opening it must be lowered at least once during every performance to ensure its being in proper working order. 4.—Smoking is not permitted in the auditorium. 5.—All gangways, passages and staircases must be kept free from chairs or any other obstructions, whether permanent or temporary.

HIS MAJESTY'S   *September 20th,* 1923

Another page from the programme of the 1923 London production.

An examination of a copy of the play which was owned by a member of the London cast shows a number of pencil alterations. The text then corresponded in many respects to Dean's published version of 1951. Dean made major changes to three scenes for his original production. Act IV Scene 1 was omitted (see Appendix III for Flecker's comment on the importance of this scene) and for Scene 2, Dean used Hassan and Ishak as the two guards — a move confirmed by the photographs of the production. The Ghost Scene which ends Act V Scene 1 was omitted for the London production. Dean directed that the Ghosts of Rafi and Pervaneh cross the stage as Hassan and Ishak exit in terror.

In Act III Scene 3, the second and third verses of the Soldiers' Song were omitted and there was an extra fanfare inserted for the Caliph's 'irrevocable judgment'. In Act V Scene 1, in order to comply with the ruling of the censor, the coffins were not brought out, nailed down and placed on the cart.

Hassan had at last reached the dress rehearsals, nine years after Dean's promise to Flecker that he would indeed stage it. The tremendous pitch of excitement and anxiety is all too clear in Dean's autobiography and it does not need much imagination to sense the atmosphere in the theatre at the penultimate rehearsal. For Dean:

'. . . these preliminaries acquired special significance in the case of *Hassan* because a new work by a distinguished composer played by an orchestra of symphony players under a brilliant young conductor, was about to be heard for the first time.' [19]

Delius attended two of the dress rehearsals, as Philip Heseltine recalls in a letter written to the composer van Dieren when he describes that Delius 'had to be carried in and out of the theatre in the Caliph's chair of state for the last day or two — but he has now got a proper contrivance on wheels, and an attendant.'

It was a dress rehearsal fraught with minor disasters — fortunately, for the superstitious. Once all the problems with the props and costumes had been sorted out, the overture began, and things continued smoothly until the first major scene-change, from Act I Scene 2, 'The Street of Felicity by the Fountain of the Two Pigeons', to Act II Scene 1, 'The House of the Moving Walls'. It is a transformation ripe for testing the skills of the most experienced theatrical technicians anywhere and this change was longer than the Prelude to Act II.

Goossens did what any conductor would surely have done — he repeated the music. At least he began to repeat it, until a screech from an irate Delius interrupted the flow: 'No, no, no, Mr Goossens. What are you doing? You musn't play it twice!' Dean and Goossens managed to pacify the composer and the rehearsal continued. [20]

Sir James Barrie sent Dean a note late after the final rehearsal: 'Tonight you will have such a night in the theatre as never again in your life.'[21]

How right he was! London's theatrical supporters were eagerly looking forward to what the *Daily Mail* called the 'event of prime literary as well as theatrical importance, and in addition there is the interest of a musical score, by Mr Frederick Delius, which promises to be far more serious than the usual interludes.'

A quarter of an hour before the play started, Delius was half-lifted from a taxi-cab outside the theatre and wheeled in an invalid chair to the stalls. As the performance commenced early, several leading theatrical figures were able to see the opening before going on to their own theatres. Standing at the back of the dress circle with Ivor Novello was Gladys Cooper, wearing a gown and closely enwrapped coat of black Marocain with a collar of chinchilla. Another was Meggie Albanesi, dressed in black, with her satin toque draped into outstanding bow-loops at the right side. Some actors and actresses made sure they left their own theatres early in order to witness the closing scene; among them were Gerald du Maurier and Dennis Eadie.

One who was able to stay the whole evening was Lady Diana Duff-Cooper, ermine-cloaked and wearing a single flower of soft mauve velvet edged with gold in her hair. Viola Tree wore a dress of parchment-shaded satin *beauté* with crystal and diamond embroideries with a Spanish shawl; Mrs Alec Rea was dressed in a cloak of turquoise blue velvet and silver and a straight-hanging gown of silver tissue brocade with a full tunic skirt of black tulle and silver with flowers at the side.

Also present were Lady Louise Mountbatten with her fiancé, the Crown Prince of Sweden (who established the Swedish translation and acting edition), Lord Lurgan, Sir Eric Geddes, Compton Mackenzie, Arnold Bennett, A A Milne, John Drinkwater, Reginald Berkeley, J M Barrie, Philip Heseltine, Beatrice Harrison, Dr and Mrs Flecker, and Mme. Flecker, who next morning sent Dean a telegram:

'. . . I must tell you again I never hoped for anything so perfectly beautiful as your production and I know for sure how much Roy would have liked it.'

Nevertheless, she maintained her watchful attitude over the play by adding:

'. . . I will come round and see you at your office one of these days. I want to tell you one or two weak points in the acting.'

Flecker's parents were in the audience but their opinion has not been recorded, except that his mother was shocked by the bare midriffs!

John Galsworthy saw the play and wrote to Dean:

'. . . I thought that for colour, design, beauty and aptness of stage-setting it surpassed anything I have seen on the English stage . . . The music is extraordinarily mediocre. You were let down there, as I thought you would be.'[22]

Galsworthy was entitled to his view but it did not deter queues forming at the box-office for a production that played to packed houses for 281 performances. It was probably *Hassan* that *The Stage* was referring to when it reported on 11 October that 'last week a musical play touched £2,400'.

It was certainly an eye-catching and colourful production, and the colour-scheme of the costumes had been carefully considered. The audience vehemently applauded the dancers and the soldiers' march, and admired the masculine characters garbed in rich brocades, opulent velvets and sumptuous silks.

The women were clad in more gossamer materials, Pervaneh in her draperies of mist blue and silver seemed ethereal by contrast with Yasmin, who first appeared framed by the green of the open doors on her balcony, aflame in robes of rose, orange and gold with a closely-draped hipsash of still deeper shadings and, bound about her head under the golden veil, other foldings of orange, with just a gleam of still more vivid jade green. Later she parted the black and silver curtains of the silver bed clad in silver tissue and Persian trousers of white satin with a patterning of blue and rose blossoms, and trailing scarves in the blended colours.

The feast of colour continued with the whirlwind bacchanalian dancers wearing swirling transparent skirts of black and gold over Persian trousers of shining gold and silver tissues. When the beggars threw away their rags they revealed splendid figures in green and gold, surrounded by crowds of girls in turquoise, silver, black and gold.

In the Palace Garden the slender branches of the almond tree were heavy with pink and white blossoms; the tall blackness of the cypress tree towered against the sky and the silver fountain ashine in the moonlight all took their place in a very well-designed production.

It was acclaimed an unqualified success and the review which pleased Dean most was from *The Daily Telegraph*, which stated: '. . . the scenic marvels had not outfaced the literary merit of the work'. He was partly proud of the fact that the work had gained the merit it deserved from the literary angle and partly glad that the advance publicity about the camels and Eastern pantomime had been inaccurate.

In fact there *were* camels present, but Harris had produced a magnificent caravan without using the real beasts! Despite Flecker's plea to Dean on 18 June 1914: '. . . Can we have *real camels* for the final scene?', Harris had cut tiny profiles out of three-ply wood, painted them himself and placed them on an eccentric track behind the distant sandhills of the last scene so that, as the pilgrims left 'The Gate of the Moon', the camel-train could be faintly seen, moving with stately pace, along 'The Golden Road to Samarkand'.[23] Lighting effects reached their height during this scene. As dawn broke, the light changed and the black and gold gates were opened. At first, nothing could be seen of the desert road, but the light continued to change, gradually revealing the dark outlines of the plain. Slowly it grew stronger and the caravan started on its way until only Hassan and Ishak remained. The sun was now shining brightly and they departed in a blaze of glory to join the caravan as it moved down the golden winding road into the valley. The caravan disappearing from sight was an ingenious device for getting it off the stage without destroying the illusion of the journey. Ainley was the last character to be seen on a now dimly-lit stage.

On the debit side, Marsh and other admirers of Flecker shuddered as various aspects of the play revealed themselves to the packed theatre. They disapproved of the fountain spurting red at the appropriate moment and they thought Dean's spectacle involved too many scene-changes and long ballets, resulting in cuts to important scenes. He cut out Act IV Scene 1, a scene considered to be of importance because it kept Hassan involved in the secondary plot in the play (even Flecker admitted that: see Appendix III) and he also cut the Ghost scene, a move which he regretted later.[24] Flecker would have been dismayed if he had seen the play with his Ghost scene cut, because he told Savery in March 1914:

'. . . [Dean] says he wouldn't dream of cutting out the Ghosts — which has reassured me vastly.'[25]

This scene is vitally important to the play and to an understanding of Flecker. It provides a link between the ghastly earthy tortures of Rafi and Pervaneh and the spiritual implications between Hassan's and Ishak's decision to take 'The Golden Road to Samarkand'. When Flecker wrote the scene in August 1913, he recalled it took him half-an-hour as he knew very clearly just what he wanted to say on the eternal question of Life and Death.[26]

Delius's impressions of the play were recorded in a letter (dictated to Jelka) he sent to Percy Grainger on 29 September 1923:

'. . . We were 9 days in London and attended 2 rehearsals and 2 performances. The whole show is really magnificent, wonderful scenery, lighting and costumes and I understand now that there really was too little music before I had written the additions, especially for the last 2 scenes, where music goes on almost all the time. The leaving of the Caravan, the gradual disappearing made a wonderful effect and was beautifully realized by the chorusses on and behind the scene. In fact all chorusses were excellent. *Our* ballet piece was a *great success* and brought just a vigorous contrast to the rest. The serenade sounded *very well* pizzicato and a muted violin playing the melody. It is then sung later on with the tenor voice and orchestra. I have discarded the Piano altogether. Afterwards it comes once more as an entr'acte for full orchestra — also very good. But of course a real artistic atmosphere is unobtainable as the public chats, drinks tea, eats chocolates as soon as the curtain drops and the actors insist on coming out after every scene, instead of only after the big acts. The piece, tho', seems to have been a very great success and the advance-booking has beaten all records of London theatres.'

'. . . P.S. In the ballet you brought in that rhythmical vigour which contrasted so well with the first part. I wish you could have heard it. It really came off splendidly.'

May Harrison recorded Delius's reactions rather differently:

'. . . he and Mrs Delius had been to see my people at the time "Hassan" was produced, which has so greatly distressed him and made him quite ill. At the first performance the audience had talked loudly through all his music, and he could hardly hear a sound of it.'[27]

Goossens recalls that Delius 'left the theatre after the performance acutely depressed by what he called that "stupid first-night audience of scatter-brains". I accompanied him and his wife to their hotel, hoping to enliven him with some champagne. But he insisted on retiring . . .'.[28]

The house-lights were dimmed after the music had begun, instead of before, which probably accounts for the audience's behaviour. A fair appraisal of Delius's contribution came from Beecham:

'. . . The success of the piece was unquestionable . . . this aesthetically pleasing and economically welcome event reacted favourably on Frederick, both mentally and physically'

and talking of this love for the theatre:

'. . . the ancient fire burns brightly for a few rare moments.'[29]

Hassan was produced in New York on 22 September 1924, reputedly losing £100,000 — a record loss for a Broadway production. Needless to say it was an unhappy memory for Dean and those so closely associated with its London success. Malone informed him that he had sold the American rights of the play to A L Erlanger, president of the Knickerbocker Theatre. The sale included everything connected with the play. Dean told Malone that 'it was a crazy arrangement' and furthermore, did his best to avert the inevitable disaster. Erlanger did not wait for Dean to become free from his London commitment in order to supervise the production and he went ahead, cutting the script considerably. The special orchestra was under the direction of Milan Roder.

The irony of the timing of that production was that Dean, Harris and Goossens were all aboard the SS *Majestic*, which sailed for New York on 17 September. Dean had no idea that the play had been produced, and together they read the press reviews on 23 September. Eugene reacted with 'My God!'; Dean's 'eyes were full of tears'; George's 'language was unprintable'.[30] The whole sad story of that production is summed up in this short newspaper paragraph:

'The imported *Hassan*, a complete failure, was withdrawn from the Knickerbocker Theatre last night after two disastrous weeks. In London, a year ago, it was a considerable success, and by duplicating the London production it was hoped also to duplicate the London success. But London, which has remained oblivious to nearly all of the theatre's progress in the past decade, proved more willing to accept an old-style production than did this town.'

FOOTNOTES

[1] George Grossmith (1874-1935): star of the Gaiety Theatre. J A E Malone: joint partner in managing His Majesty's Theatre.

[2] Dean, *op cit*, p179.

[3] *Ibid*, p182. The piano score referred to is the arrangement made by Philip Heseltine of Delius's original music composed in 1920. It was published by Universal Edition.

[4] Eugene Goossens (1893-1962): English composer and conductor. His brother Leon and sister Sidonie played in the orchestra for *Hassan*, which he conducted for the first night, prior to Percy Fletcher taking over.

[5] Goossens, *op cit*, p209.

[6] Dean, *op cit*, p146.

[7] Philip Heseltine (1894-1930). British writer and composer (under the pseudonym of Peter Warlock), influenced by his friend Delius, of whom he wrote the first biography.

[8] Radio broadcast by Dean, 3 July 1968.

[9] Wife of Henry Clews, an American sculptor who met Delius in 1913 and shared his outlook and philosophy.

[10] Flecker's own stage directions sound very simple and very effective: 'Intones to the accompaniment of the lute.'

[11] It was some of this that was later composed by Percy Grainger (see Chapter 7).

[12] Sherwood, *op cit*, p207.

[13] T. E. Lawrence (1888-1935): author of *The Seven Pillars of Wisdom*.

[14] Sherwood, *op cit*, pxvi, xvii, 22, 146.

[15] Dean, *op cit*, p184.

[16] *Ibid*, p172-3.

[17] Roger Ould: Dean's personal assistant, and Willie Warde, the veteran pantomimist.

[18] Dean's introduction to *Hassan* (Heinemann Drama Library, 1951, p xix). Flecker also believed in this. 'Plays are hardly ever published before they are acted. It's dangerous for one thing.'

[19] Dean, *op cit*, p186.

[20] *Ibid*, p187.

[21] Sir James Barrie (1860-1937): journalist and biographer, but best remembered as a dramatist and author of *Peter Pan*. Dean, *op cit*, p187.

[22] John Galsworthy (1867-1933): novelist and dramatist. *The Forsyte Saga, Strife* and *The Skin Game* are well-known examples, Dean, *op cit*, p189-90. When I questioned Dean further about his reaction to Delius's music, he simply said that Galsworthy was very conventional and did not consider Delius a suitable composer for the play.

[23] Dean, *op cit*, p189.

[24] *Radio Times*, 31 October 1952.

[25] *Some Letters From Abroad*, *op cit*, p144.

[26] Sherwood, *op cit*, p188.

[27] From *The Royal College of Music Magazine*, May 1937, No. 2 (reprinted in *A Delius Companion*, ed. Christopher Redwood, John Calder, 1976).

[28] Goossens, *op cit*, p210.

[29] Beecham, *op cit*, p193, p221. Readers' attention is drawn to the inaccurate date which Beecham gives for the performance at Darmstadt. On page 199 he states it was 1927, but there is no evidence to suggest that the play was mounted there again.

[30] Dean, *op cit*, p234.

Chapter 7

A NOTE ON THE MUSIC

by CHRISTOPHER REDWOOD

As has been indicated in the foregoing chapters, Delius worked on the music for *Hassan* in two main phases: first, in 1920, in response to Dean's original commission, and second, between 19 June and 4 August 1923, when Dean realised that more music was required. There are consequently two manuscript full-scores, and piano reductions by Philip Heseltine of both of these were published. The earlier consisted of 40 pages and was dated 'FD 1920'; the later was 67 pages long and marked 'FD 1920-23'. Each was published by Universal Edition, and in 1965 Boosey and Hawkes, who had taken over the copyright, published a version musically identical to the later one. It is unfortunate that the second piano score, unlike its predecessor, was not provided with cues for the musical interjections.

The manuscript full-score of the earlier version, which runs to 127 pages, is in the possession of the Delius Trust. It is partly in mauve ink and partly blue-black, the latter having been identified as the hand of Philip Heseltine. Under the mauve ink the composer's pencil can be detected (see example on page 49). The German translation of the stage and tempo directions are in Jelka's hand, and she has also been responsible for some of the names of instruments and clefs. There are two manuscript full-scores of the later version, both of which are in the hand of unidentified copyists, and do not incorporate Jelka's '52 big pages';[1] the whereabouts of these is at present unknown.

The present publisher also houses a set of orchestral parts which corresponds to the earlier full-score. These are liberally sprinkled with pencilled instructions in German, which leave little doubt that they were used at Darmstadt in June 1923. Any criticism of the music at that production should, therefore, be read with the understanding that it was the first version that was played.

That it was inadequate in quantity can be seen from the fact that several parts had to be repeated: the final six bars of the opening Prelude were one example, and the second appearance of the 'Street of Felicity' music was another, while the fanfare was played no less than 13 times (this presumably necessitated by the longer Leysin Version of the play which was being used). On the other hand, the Prelude to Act V, Scene 2 was truncated by the removal of its first 42 bars.

One interesting point is that the first full-score does not exhibit any

74

German adumbrations, nor for that matter does it show signs of having been used by a conductor at any time. Two conjectures seem plausible: either the conductor at Darmstadt, Herr Rosenstock, preferred to conduct from a piano score, or he used another full-score which has since been lost.

Having realised that there was not sufficient music at Darmstadt, Dean requested additions 'from a loudly protesting composer'. Philip Heseltine enumerated these in an interesting article published in *The Daily Telegraph* on 23 September 1923. The serenade, originally conceived as a tenor vocalise behind the scenes with piano accompaniment and harp ritornelli, was rearranged as a muted violin solo with pizzicato string accompaniment and harp; later it was sung to the same accompaniment, and finally, it was played in a richly scored version as an interlude between the first and second scenes (scenes 2 and 3 in the 1922 edition) of Act III where there was originally a 9-bar truncated version of the serenade. The unaccompanied chorus behind the scenes was transferred from Act II to Act I, Scene 2. The accompanied female chorus in Act II ('Daughters of Delight') was extended considerably, as were the introduction and ending of the men's chorus ('We are they who come faster than fate'). New music was also written for the interlude between scenes 1 and 2 of Act I (based on the 'Street of Felicity' motif), the last movement of the ballet in Act II, the unaccompanied chorus after the moving walls have descended, the music to accompany Ishak's poem, and the interlude between scenes 1 and 2 of Act IV. The introduction to the last scene was also extended (by the addition of the tenor's vocalise and the passage that follows), and the final chorus, originally for male voices only, was rearranged for mixed chorus: a move which works well musically if not dramatically. Finally, the original Prelude to Act V was used instead as an introduction to Act II, Scene 2 in place of the 'Street of Felicity' music.

Account must also be taken of two vocal scores of *Hassan* which are signed by Basil Dean and Percy Fletcher respectively. As would be expected, each is of the 1920 version heavily interleaved with additional music on manuscript paper. They do not correspond exactly, but a careful correlation of the two gives us a fairly reliable picture of what music was actually played in the theatre. As a result, it is not entirely surprising to discover that just as the text differed considerably from the printed version, so the music was also not exactly as published. For instance, the dance in which Percy Grainger lent a hand (*vide infra*) was ironically shorn of its opening 39 bars, actually starting at the tenth bar of page 29 of the later vocal score, in the section written by Grainger. Later, when the music returns to that composed by Delius, the section from the top of page 31 to the fourth bar of page 32 was played twice over.

In addition to the alterations already mentioned there were many modifications to the score. Starting from the beginning, the Prelude to Act I was lengthened by 7 bars: two bars of harp followed by the descending 'Golden Road' theme played softly on the clarinet (These notes can be heard on Percy Fletcher's recording of the work, referred to later). During the playing of the Prelude Henry Ainley, who took the part of Hassan, recited the first four verses of Flecker's prologue *The Golden Journey to Samarkand* behind an illuminated tableau curtain, and someone evidently had the notion of adding these notes to coincide with the final line. The interlude between scenes 1 and 2 of the first Act was deprived of its opening two bars, and was marked 'repeat if necessary'. The Prelude to Act II was replaced by the 'Street of Felicity' music, followed by the vocal version of the Serenade and rounded off with a repeat of the interlude between Act I, scenes 1 and 2. The 'Street of Felicity' music was not played at the beginning of Act II, scene 2, presumably because it had been heard twice already. New fanfares were provided to announce the appearance of the Chief of Police and the Captain of the Military in that scene; at the Caliph's exit a new eleven-bar sequence, based on the Prelude to Act I, was inserted. The serenade was heard for the third time at the end of Act III, scene 1, and additional fanfares were provided for Act III, scene 2. The curtain to Act IV rose on scene 2, thus rendering the interlude between the two scenes superfluous. Instead it was played as an introduction to Act V, beginning at bar 15. The Procession of Protracted Death was evidently found too short to cover the whole business, for it is marked 'repeat ad lib.', the signal for its ending being a yawn from Masrur! Finally, the Prelude to Act I, starting at the third line, was added to the introduction to the Ghost Scene. The whole musical score was played at His Majesty's Theatre as follows:

Act I	Prelude with recitation.
	Interlude between scenes 1 and 2. Cue — Hassan: 'Did I not say "They shall be flowers?"'
	Introduction to scene 2 (page 6, lower).
	Serenade. Cue — Hassan: '. . . and enchant the dropping stones? Ah, Yasmin?'
	Page 8 (lower). Cue — Hassan: 'Farewell, and the Salaam!'
	Pages 9-10. Cue — Ishak: '. . . in the shape of that tall cypress that has leapt the wall to shoot her arrow at the stars?'
	Page 8 (lower) repeated. Cue — Ishak: 'I come, my master!' Join to:
	Repeat of Serenade, with tenor behind scenes or in orchestra. Join to:
	Repeat of Interlude between scenes 1 and 2.
Act II	Fanfare (page 12, bottom line). Cue — Rafi: 'Ho, music! Ho, dancers!'
	Dance of the Beggars. Cue — Caliph: '. . . what shapely legs, what jasmine arms!' Join to:

Chorus of Women. Join to:

Divertissement.

General Dance (page 29, bar 10 onwards. Repeat page 31 to bar 4 of page 32). Cue — Chorus: 'Paradox in Paradise'.

Chorus of Beggars and Dancing Girls. Cue — Rafi and chorus: 'Answered!'

Prelude to Act V. Cue — Caliph: 'Hassan, I will join thee: thou art a man of taste.'

Fanfare (14 bars not printed). Cue — Ali: 'I never meddle in politics'.

Fanfare (8 bars not printed). Cue — Yasmin: '. . . for frail-as-a-rose ladies in danger's hour'.

Music accompanying Ishak's poem. Cue — Jafar: 'Thy dawn, O Master!'

Exit of Caliph (11 bars not printed). Cue — Bearers: 'Ready, Lord and Master'.

Act III   Prelude.

Repeat of Serenade. Cue — Hassan: 'Yasmin!' Join to:

Chorus of Soldiers.

Fanfare (page 43, bottom line). Cue — Captain of Military: 'Allah, these Poets talk in rhyme!'

Fanfare (not printed). Cue — Ishak: '. . . and escape the formalities of the court'.

Entry of the Caliph. Cue — Dervish: '. . . a plaything, a shadow, the Caliph!'

Fanfare (not printed). Cue — Caliph: 'I will speak plain and clear'.

Fanfare (not printed). Cue — Caliph: '. . . the Divan is closed'.

Act IV   Prelude.

Interlude between scenes 1 and 2 (beginning bar 15). Cue — Rafi: 'Death!'

Act V   Song of the Muezzin.

Procession of Protracted Death. Cue — Yasmin: 'I shall see it all!'

Prelude to last scene. Cue — Ishak: 'Follow the bells!' Join to:

Prelude to Act I (omitting first two lines of music). Join to:

Closing scene.

Heseltine also states that the whole of the 1923 additional music was dictated to Jelka as Delius was unable to hold a pen at this time. In point of fact, she was not the only person to help, as there is proof that Percy Grainger actually composed a short section of the music. In 1936, Grainger wrote to Eric Fenby: 'It was not *the scoring* of Hassan I helped him with. He wanted 3 minutes (about) more music for a ballet section, and this I composed and scored (I forget whether I used any of his themistic material, or not)'. According to Grainger's biographer, John Bird, this took place between 21 July and 8 August 1923, when the Australian composer was staying with the Deliuses at their Norwegian house. Delius 'decided to ask his friend to write a dance movement for inclusion in the final work. On the basis of a tune given to him by Delius, he therefore sketched several pages for what was eventually included in the score as *Allgemeiner Tanz* ('General Dance'). Delius himself later filled out the instrumentation and completed the movement.'[2] Grainger's contribution has been identified as pages 28 (line 3) — 33 of the second vocal score.[3] The last section of this returns to Delius's earlier part of the dance, but the central section, with the tenors' direction 'very nasal and strident', sounds more like Grainger than Delius. That Grainger played a part in the composition is verified by Delius's letter to him reproduced in Chapter 6, which also indicates his satisfaction with the result.

Philip Heseltine drew attention to some similarities in the score of *Hassan* to moments in other works by Delius, a feature which will come as no surprise to those who know the music of this composer. Perhaps the most striking is the appearance of one of the best-known leitmotifs from *A Village Romeo and Juliet* in the middle of the interlude between Scenes 1 and 2 of Act IV. The reminiscence was probably unconscious, but the emotions are similar: Rafi and Pervaneh have just chosen to die together; Sali and Vrenchen are to make the same choice.

The other similarity pointed out by Heseltine is between the motif associated with the Fountain of the Two Pigeons in the 'Street of Felicity' and the theme of the slow movement of the First Violin Sonata and the coda of the 'Cello Sonata. To this we may add that the melody for brass in the central section of the Prelude to Act I bears some resemblance to the leitmotif associated with Koanga in the opera of that name. There are many other little Delius 'fingerprints' to be found, in the form of short four- or five-note melismas, usually in quavers or semiquavers.

At the time of writing, there is no recording of the complete *Hassan* music, the fullest being one side of a record made by Sir Thomas Beecham in 1955.[4] Intending producers who are without the services of an orchestra may like to note that although this record contains only about 20 minutes of music, with judicious use it can provide quite an effective musical accompaniment to the play. The music contained on this record, in the order it is played, is as follows. Page numbers refer to the later vocal score:

1 Interlude between Scenes 1 and 2 of Act 1 (page 5).
2 Serenade (violin solo) (page 7).
3 Interlude where Hassan falls by the fountain (page 8, last six bars only).

4   Unaccompanied wordless chorus behind the scenes (page 9).
5   Ballet of the Beggars (page 13).
6   Entrance of the fair and dusky beauties (abbreviated) (page 18).
7   Chorus of Women from Act II (page 19).
8   Prelude to Act III (page 37).
9   Introduction and chorus of soldiers from Act III (page 40).
10   Procession of Protracted Death (page 50).
11   Reprise of Serenade, but solo viola instead of violin.
12   Closing scene.

Beecham made several previous recordings of parts of the music. In 1934 he made a 78 rpm disc of what he called *Intermezzo and Serenade from Hassan*, the intermezzo being that between Act I, Scenes 1 and 2. In 1938 he recorded the closing scene, a peculiar record in which he allowed the tenor soloist to sing the semiquavers as quavers (thus altering the whole rhythm of the piece), hastened the music somewhat towards the end of the introduction, and then almost doubled speed for 'We take the Golden Road'.[5] In his 1955 version the tenor sang in the correct rhythm, and the final chorus was taken at about two-thirds of the speed of the earlier recording. Basil Dean criticised the later one as 'too somnolent', saying that he had ended his stage presentation 'on a note of almost religious fervour'.

The only other extended recording of the *Hassan* music was made on two 78 rpm discs in 1923 by the Chorus and Orchestra of His Majesty's Theatre, conducted by Percy Fletcher.[6] These records are of interest as they contain some passages which have not been recorded elsewhere, but they would not be suitable for use in conjunction with a modern presentation of the play. The excerpts, in order of playing, are:

1   Prelude to Act I.
2   Serenade (tenor solo with pizzicato strings and harp).
3   The Beggars' Song from Act II.
4   The entrance of the fair and dusky beauties.
5   General Dance from Act II (from the ¾ allegro).
6   Prelude to Act 5, last 9 bars omitted, and leading to:
7   Procession of Protracted Death.
8   Orchestral introduction to chorus of soldiers (Act III).
9   Final chorus, from where the voices enter in four-parts.

In the final chorus the words are not repeated continuously, as indicated in the score, but are interspersed with Hassan's verse:

'Sweet to ride forth at evening from the wells,
    When shadows press gigantic on the sand,
And softly through the silence beat the bells,
    Along the Golden Road to Samarkand.'

This also may have been performed in the theatre. The voice parts do not end the Act III Bacchanale with a shout, but singing the notes indicated in the score. According to a review in *The Gramophone*,[7] this normally took the sopranos up to somewhere near top B, but although this and a portamento were tried in the studio, the recording equipment was not sufficiently sensitive to reproduce it satisfactorily, and a compromise had to be arrived at. Although it is well-known that recording managers sometimes persuaded conductors to speed up in those days in order to accommodate the music on one side of a 78 rpm disc, these records may be taken as giving some indication of the way in which the music was executed at His Majesty's. The *Daughters of Delight* chorus is certainly much too fast, losing all poetry, and the serenade loses something for a similar reason. In general, all of the music is taken faster than we are used to hearing it, although the final chorus is not as quick as Beecham's 1938 version.

The complete music was played in a BBC broadcast of the play, first heard on 23rd December 1973. The production was by Raymond Raikes, and the music played by the BBC Welsh Orchestra, conducted by Rae Jenkins. Sections which were not played in context, such as the ballet music, were heard as an appendix. This recording is not available commercially.

While this is not the place to attempt a detailed analysis of the music for *Hassan*, a few general remarks may not be without interest. Delius was not a composer who found favour when music was commissioned. The highly individual nature of his music and his personal aloofness saw to that, and in fact he was probably only commissioned to write one or two other works during his whole career. Where music for the stage was concerned, it is notable that he chose his own stories and usually fashioned his own libretti. By this means he was able to concentrate upon scenes which appealed to his muse, and avoid as much as possible those that did not. (Thus did he come to divide his last opera, *Fennimore and Gerda*, into a series of poetic tone pictures, connected by orchestral intermezzi — a novel idea for the opera-house).

With a commission such as *Hassan*, he was required to provide music at prescribed moments, irrespective of whether the mood of the story appealed to him at these points. We should therefore expect to find a certain amount of music that was uncharacteristic of the composer. Nevertheless it is safe to say that he would certainly have found the story in general one with which he was in complete sympathy, particularly the abbreviated love-affair of Rafi and Pervaneh. Had he been writing an opera he would have made a marvellous musical translation of the Ghost scene with its implied denial of life-after-death.

It should also be remembered that he was writing for a theatrical audience rather than an assembly of concert-goers. To this end he was shrewd enough to include what has become one of his most popular melodies, the Serenade. The fact that he repeated it twice in the 1923 version of the score indicates that he himself realised its potential.

He was also wise enough to avoid the normal methods employed by theatrical composers when required to provide music for eastern settings: the use of pentatonic and whole-tone scales. Delius manages much more effectively with nothing more exotic than the harmonic minor. The unaccompanied chorus in Act I is in his most inspired manner: a virtually atonal poem of beauty, which deserves to be included in recitals of his other unaccompanied part-songs.

The 'Street of Felicity' motif and the intermezzo between Scenes 1 and 2 of the first Act are also in his happiest style. To these may be added the music to accompany Ishak's poem, and the Prelude to Act III (Who but Delius would have composed a theatrical prelude which included wordless female voices?).

Generally speaking, the faster sections, such as the chorus of beggars and the ballet music, are not characteristic of the composer, and as to the soldier's song, 'We are they who come faster than fate', one can only say that Flecker would probably have been furious at the insensitive way that the words of his most famous poem had been handled. The chorus of fair and dusky beauties is noteworthy for its basic melody, which consists of nothing more than a descending chromatic scale: a feature not uncommon in Delius's music, although more often encountered in the bass. Attention is also drawn to some cross-references, such as the theme of the opening music in the closing bars of the Prelude to Act V, the notes of this melody itself being identical to the opening of the Soldiers' Chorus.

In conclusion, it should be mentioned that in 1929, Eric Fenby prepared a choral suite from the *Hassan* music, apparently at the suggestion of Balfour Gardiner. Originally the following excerpts appeared in the order given: Prelude to Act I; Prelude to Act II and Ballet; Serenade (with solo 'cello); Procession of Protracted Death; Closing Scene (from p. 56 of later vocal score). The Preludes to Acts I and II were later removed, and the remaining excerpts played in the reverse order.

The most interesting feature of this arrangement is that Delius instructed Fenby to score it for full orchestra, with two each of flutes, clarinets, bassoons and trumpets, four horns and three trombones. It may be conjectured that this was the sort of orchestra that the composer originally had in mind for the incidental music.

(see page 82 for footnote)

FOOTNOTES

[1] See p61.

[2] John Bird, *Percy Grainger* (Elek Books, 1976) p183.

[3] For this and earlier information concerning original scores the writer is indebted to Rachel Lowe: *A Catalogue of the Music Archive of the Delius Trust* (Boosey & Hawkes, 1974), pp167-8.

[4] This monaural recording has been issued three times, the respective numbers being: Fontana CFL1020, Philips GL5691, and CBS61224.

[5] This recording has recently been transferred to LP and reissued in a five-record box, *The Music of Delius*, SHB32. The set also contains the 1934 recording of the Intermezzo and Serenade referred to, and the unaccompanied chorus from Act I, recorded in the same year.

[6] C11134/5.

[7] February 1924.

APPENDIX I

REVIEWS OF THE
DARMSTADT PRODUCTION

Darmstädter Tagblatt, 2 June 1923
'Hassan'

'The story of Hassan of Bagdad and how he came to take the golden road to Samarkand is the narrative from the *Thousand and one Nights*. This method is not new on the German stage; long ago Max Reinhardt very successfully presented the pantomime *Sumurun*, which accurately struck the oriental style in its contents and the presentation of the characters. The same cannot be said of *Hassan*. The outer frame depicts one of the reputed revolts against the caliph Harun al Rashid. Hassan is a simple confectioner who by accident is lucky enough to save the caliph's life, and who is rewarded for this with the highest honour, as a result of which, however, things do not go well for him and he eventually leaves the wicked city of Bagdad. This basic plot is told with still further happenings interwoven; an abundance of pretty fantasies and amorous scenes mix with cruelty and aesthetic contemplation. Eroticism and sadism stand in the foreground and to this end there are many fine scenes skilfully put together, which contain neither much spirit nor much art, but which are extraordinarily rewarding to a skilful director. And so the direction of Herr Hartung tonight celebrated an orgy. Just as his art in producing the works of the classical German theatre did not always strike the right note, this oriental art is exactly in his line. That it was no oriental legend suited well the work itself, which seems to have been written only for directors and stage-machinery. The art-form, as it has been produced, deserves the highest praise. There were stage pictures of the most fascinating beauty; the intimate charm of narrow, moonlit streets, the solemn meeting at the divan, the caliph's magnificent garden, and so on; only the 'most beautiful fountain in the world' which is shown there was an ugly misrepresentation. Costumes, colours and lighting all struck the right note in keeping with the whole stage-picture, and the eye found much delight. In addition, the ear was flattered by the music written for it by Delius, which by providing a prelude to each individual scene led one along with its oriental sounds.

The drama, which surely by its contents ought to come over only in a dreamlike way as in a legend, has a disturbingly harsh effect with its crass and dramatic scenes. The wild outburst of feeling in the prison, which tears at the nerves in an unsuitable way, would perhaps have been better conceived as a lyric scene, as well as the dreadful torture scene which, with its hooded men and torture-instruments, reminds one of the inquisition, ultimately severely weakened the effect of the play. Because of the length (the production lasted five hours) several cuts were necessary; the most offensive parts were not included, but regrettably the humourous scene between the two beggars had to fall by the wayside, as did also the closing scene in the park, and also the whole last scene at the city gate, which gives the piece a reconciliatory, and therefore poetic, ending.

The theatrical presentation was all of the highest order. The confectioner Hassan was in every way the best role Herr Valk has undertaken. So quite magically comprehended was this odious, enamoured old man that through all the drastic events he was at no time laughable but managed to be strongly and purely human. Especially in the first scene in his dwelling and then his greatest performance: the love-duet on the balcony. There Herr Valk allowed the full range of his art to play; his awkward walk and his always expressive posture, controlled as much as his voice, from the warm tones of the heart to the wild outburst of despair. His false friend Selim was played by Herr Hölzlin, who also emerged as a fine actor throughout this rôle. Harun al Rashid was not only the wise and upright caliph of the orient as the Frankish historian would have us believe, but also a cruel tyrant. Thus was he depicted by Flecker and thus was he played by Herr Rehmer, who combined refined peace and loftiness with despotic harshness. His attendants, Ishak, Jafar and Masrur, were given by Herren Gielen, Sebald and Langheinz with excellent characterisation and good appearances. Outstanding here was the precious Chinese woven garment that Herr Gielen wore. Herr Kulisch had the large part of the king of the beggars; he was at his best in the peaceful aspects of his rôle, and the speech where he has the caliph as an unrecognised guest. The later passionate outbursts are too highly dramatic and too highly pitched for the tone of the play. The same goes for his partner, Fräulein Sanzara, who played the lovely Pervaneh with all her charm and with animated passion. In Fräulein Lisso, who as a guest played Yasmin, we became acquainted with an artist of great ability. She presented a good, advantageous appearance, well-produced voice with clear speech and rounded, well-thought-out acting; so her rendering as the seductive young widow was a very successful performance. Next to the many other contributory parts, outstanding were the beautiful song of the Meuzzin (Herr Hoefflin), Herr Schneider as the herald, who through good and lively diction offered a beautiful performance of his difficult rôle, and also Herren Baumeister and Schütz as officers. The four young slaves were played just so-so by four ladies of the ballet; the squeaks of the smallest always provoked laughter. There was also dancing and belly-dancing. In short, there was something for everyone, so everyone had to be satisfied. Or so it should have been. One has noted many beautiful things in themselves, but having done so there remains an ugly afterthought: was it really art? Indisputably there was great theatrical direction, as formerly in *Kean*; from the acting point of view it was partly great art, but from the literary angle only make-believe. And therefore it was a shame that so much trouble had been taken over this piece. But the production as such is certainly worth seeing.

There was great applause for the artists between acts and at the end — however, as was easily perceptible, not from the majority of the audience, but again and again provoked by a small claque.'

In 1923 the *Frankfurter Zeitung* was edited by Dr Heinrich Simon, a great friend and champion of Delius. It is not surprising therefore that the paper's critic, Bernhard Diebold, began his notice on 2 June by discussing the music. The following comprises almost half of his account:

'It is certainly no accident that a composer such as Frederick Delius was called upon for this musical fable. For the 'tale of Hassan of Bagdad and how he came to take the golden road to Samarkand' . . . this colourful story is in the long run much less of a poetic drama than an opera-text. And indeed such a very, very long opera-text that one would not term it a libretto but would without any worry call it a complete libro; a libro of such volume that in its unset state it already almost reaches the length of *Die Meistersinger*. Delius has therefore merely contented himself with music before, between, beside and after the scenes; he has created for the poor vocabulary of the author and his translators (E. W. Freissler and Herbert Alberti) with his poetic voice a dense atmosphere and lyrical background. Music for twilight, melancholy as it illustrates and accompanies the action; when it is evening; when a serenade is heard; when the beggars bay or the dancing-girls whirl; when the pomp of the divan unfolds; when the lovers soar in highest ecstasy; or when the hangman's procession parades horrifically. The monotony of the sounds, the nearly always close-set harmonies, the muffled dissonances of the chorus, the short steps of the themes, the somewhat oppressive colours of the woodwind — yielded (in the subtle presentation of conductor Rosenstock) a world of story-book melancholy which told rather in nordic than oriental style of the thousand and one nights . . .'

The critic of the *Volksfreund* (5 June 1923) opened his account:

'James Elroy Flecker, or the thwarted poet. His piece bears the sub-title: *The Story of Hassan of Bagdad and how he came to take the golden road to Samarkand*. One should first ask the question, how did the author come to take the thorny way into the theatre? In any case there were many shorter paths than the musical spectacle, namely the cinema, the opera or — if we wish to remain with literature — the novel (then he would, of course, not have come to the theatre). This, however, results in his poetic hindrance. In this almost five-hour production of a shortened spectacle there is a scene 'in the house of the moving walls': this is done to perfection in the American adventure film — with Eddie Polo or Goliath Armstrong; then a big scene in the divan of the caliph Harun al Rashid: this would have been a fabulous operatic scene — the palace-guard sing triumphal choruses anyway; or the 'procession of protracted death': this is nerve-tickling like a circus show. If a glowing, violent passion was behind it one could say that the piece blasts the theatre; Flecker, however, in spite of all difficulties, does not reach it; he remains everywhere standing in front of the stage. We are so advanced today that we instinctively perceive a sure stage-atmosphere and theatrical voice. We can mark out the atmosphere of the theatre; that Flecker does not have this sure grip probably goes together with his Englishness. A German would hardly have attempted the conquest of the theatre in this way, a romantic person never. (The French today still consider Shakespeare as stage-blasting.) The piece retains always something of a fancy-dress ball; the oriental heaviness, lasciviousness and sweetness, the music — pregnant, fruit-laden, something which in the tale from *A Thousand and One Nights* flows full and broadly, has not come over with translation into drama; the speech has breadth but no fullness, the words are linked, not grown together . . .'

A final paragraph concerning the music was added by another critic:

'For the stage-play described above all sorts of music had been provided, in front of and behind the stage, with and without mutes, sung and played. It is by Frederick Delius. The now sixty-year-old composer is rather an international mixture, in short a cross between Greig and Debussy. But an extremely cultivated one who has hardly experienced an original turn from his second homeland, America. The composer was born in England of German parents. One therefore classes him with the impressionists. This does not mean much except maybe that he ought to be able to write accompanying music for *Hassan* which suits the mood of the play. I am, however, in no position to verify this because the play did not arouse any emotions in me that might be comparable. I can only state that I heard a decent, subtle and sometimes interesting, i.e. mentally tense, composition which, however, does not seem to be representative for the entire oeuvre of the well-known composer. Rosenstock conducted; Hoefflin's voice floated sometimes over the scenery, also ladies Bass, Boerckel, Doepner and Stefanowa could be heard. Finally, the choir marched in difficult intervals and steps over the stage. It seems clear that it was no obligation to new music.'

APPENDIX II

REVIEWS OF THE
LONDON PRODUCTION

The drama writer of *The Weekly Westminster Gazette* wrote in the issue of 29 September 1923:

'If there were any doubt as to the greatness of Flecker's *Hassan* in the minds of those people who are at once too cautious to form final opinions by themselves, and too unparrot-like to repeat the louder cries of less prudent men, it may well be dispelled this week by a consideration of the many and various meanings read into the play by all the people concerned in its production at His Majesty's Theatre, and by the critics, amateur and professional, who have reported on it in print and by word of mouth since last Thursday. No two people are in complete agreement either about the play or about its performance. But everybody reads into Flecker's work some significance or other, and sees a great part of that significance well interpreted on the stage. And these diversities unite to form one tribute. None but a vitally great work, well performed, can produce either so general an enthusiasm or so much sporadic dissatisfaction as appears in the sum of these criticisms. The content of *Hassan*, like, though less than, that of *Hamlet*, can never be exhausted on the stage in one interpretation.

To begin with, we know that *Hassan*, which certain literary critics have been assuring us for years is the greatest English poetic play since *The Tempest*, has impressed Mr George Grossmith and Mr J. A. E. Malone as a business proposition. They have felt it safe to secure so distinguished a composer as Mr Frederick Delius, together with Mr Michel Fokine, a choreograph of international reputation, and Mr Basil Dean, one of the finest of living producers, to co-operate in preparing Flecker for presentation. Further, Mr Henry Ainley, who is fastidious as a great actor must be in the choice and rejection of the characters he undertakes, has thrown himself with ardour into the part of the confectioner of Bagdad, and is making of it one of the greatest, possibly quite the greatest, of all his interpretations.

This unusual agreement between the prophets of art and the priests of business is in itself a portent and cause for hope. *Hassan*, which is literature, has been put on the stage as lavishly as *Chu Chin Chow*, which was drivel, and with far more taste and regard for art and artistry in the execution of all its accessories. We have no longer to mourn the squandering of thousands of pounds for that which is not drama. Whether the honour done to Flecker has involved doing anything like justice to his work is a matter on which I, among other readers of the play, am more than a little dubious.

For we now come to the critical opinions evoked by this production. A few voices without much authority have shouted their bedazzled joy over the gorgeous spectacle, their relief that a 'high-brow' play has been made so tolerable to their perceptive faculty. Other more interesting criticism is divided, some finding that the splendour of the scene obliterates the meaning of the drama, some that its significance is enhanced when translated into material form with the detailed realism for which Mr Basil Dean has so unique a gift.

But it is in their statements of the actual content and purport of the play that the critics differ most, and by their very differences pay the most eloquent tribute to the play itself, and to the mind of the young dramatist who expressed in it his profoundest feeling about man's life and destiny.

Some people find the play divided into two contrasting parts, seeing the story of Hassan's bitter, disillusioned love for Yasmin, the beautiful woman of the town, set against that of the faithful, idealistic lovers Rafi and Pervaneh, who chose torture and death rather than life and separation. These people express some disappointment at the lack of dramatic conflict between the two intellectually conflicting tales. Others, and I find these more difficult to follow, make Hassan's adventures from the moment he sees Yasmin until the moment of his setting out to make the Golden Journey a complete philosophic allegory, in which Rafi, Pervaneh, Ishak, and the Caliph are mere illustrative arguments.

I myself have another, and I think a more dramatically unifying view of the play. *Hassan*, as I see it, has for its central figure and mainspring the Caliph, cause and author of all its action, the one character who remains unchanged throughout the play, the artist to whom 'agony is a fine colour,' the triumphant symbol of the cruelty of material beauty. Hassan, the baker with the soul of a child, is the subject of the play, the creature who is broken but not destroyed, either by Yasmin (earthly love) or by the Caliph (earthly splendour). The Caliph can torture and kill Rafi and Pervaneh, and can drive them out into the darkness where there is no remembrance. He can say to the tender, compassionate Hassan, 'You dreamt that your walls were sweating blood. I will fulfil the prophecy implied and make the dream come true.' He is the Prince of this world, and there is only one old dervish to mutter gloomily, 'A clay thing, a plaything, a shadow, the Caliph.' But he cannot destroy Hassan's love for poetry and beautiful carpets.

On the character of this tyrant Flecker has spent a wealth of language, and for him has invented a series of effects which give the play its highest dramatic value. And it is by the very gorgeousness of this sinister show of beauty and colour that the part of Hassan should by contrast be tested and magnified. The Caliph is a royal artist in life. He chooses the lowly Hassan for one of his exquisite experiments, and his victim yields him the finest responses. But the Caliph *is* a great artist, and it is here that I feel Mr Basil Dean's wonderfully planned production does not reach the full height of perfection it deserves to attain. For he has made his Caliph a subordinate figure-head, a rather cold and cruel gentleman who wears wonderful Persian clothes and speaks his coloured English lines with a clipped precision and a purity of accent which should be a lesson to some of his fellow-actors, but which is hopelessly inadequate as an enunciation of the Caliph's subtle felinities and capricious dangerousness. Mr Dean has marked this under-rating of the Caliph's importance by allowing him to be played by Mr Malcolm Keen. And Mr Keen, so admirable in the harmless necessary parts to which only a good actor can give verisimilitude, is quite incapable of suggesting the perverted romantic imagination, the magnificent Oriental cruelty of this character. He is dull where he should be vivid, violent when he should be slow and menacing. To take one instance only. Ishak, about to suffer execution, with poetic calm recites a poem and softens his master's mood. 'Sheathe your sword, Masrur,' says the Caliph to his headsman. And then, because he must still be terrifying, 'Would'st thou kill my friend?' This is a silky threat, an implied transfer of the death sentence from the courtier to the slave; it should be suavely given, an icy jest. Mr Keen shouts it in Britannic anger, and the whole character of the Caliph collapses in a phrase.

Again, the magnificent scene in the Great Hall of the Palace, superbly set and filled by Mr Fokine and Mr Dean with ballets and processions all mounting up to the climax of the Caliph's entry, for which the dramatist has prepared every ounce of effect, gives forth a most mouselike and unregal Mr Keen at the moment when 'the Drinker of Blood, the Maker of Spells, Peacock of the World,' at last makes the appearance which should take our breath with dread. Such a Caliph as Flecker saw would have paused and prepared his audience for the terrible vengeance on the King of Beggars for which the Divan has been assembled. And an actor capable of suggesting the sinister yet attractive personality of this autocrat would at every point enhance the marvel of Mr Ainley's childlike, wistful, grotesque, and adorable Hassan. As it is, the scenes with the Caliph, when Hassan should be at his greatest, all flag a little, and it is in the Pavilion scene, a piece of the perfectest comedy that Mr Ainley, discovering 'an elephant — his head only,' in his new and beautiful carpet, and finally succumbing to the wiles of the treacherous, the mercenary Yasmin, reaches his finest heights. But here he has Miss Cathleen Nesbitt, perfectly cast as Yasmin, and more beautiful in her poses and her speech than she has ever been, who gives Mr Ainley great acting to match and to enhance his own.

I would not be ungracious or ungrateful for the privilege of seeing *Hassan* acted. Even with the cuts, which have been made with real intelligence, though they must be deplored as vitiating the full meaning of the play, this production of *Hassan* is so fine that it might be tremendous, if it had not, in my opinion, missed its greatest possibility. But in detail, there are many delights. I did not care for Mr Gill's Rafi and Miss Cowie's Pervaneh. They were too mature for the passionate illusions they represent, and their parts should be played by children, or at least Pervaneh should. Miss Meggie Albanesi might make her almost unbearably poignant in lovely youth and innocent courage. But Mr Andrew Leigh's Abdu, Mr Ivor Barnard's Chinese philosopher, and the impressive Herald of Mr Douglas Burbidge, were all as good as they could be, and are only three of many small, wonderful excellencies which go to make up the fine but not quite satisfying whole of the production.'

The *Gazette's* music critic, Philip Heseltine, wrote in the same issue:

'By his happy choice of Frederick Delius as composer of the incidental music, Mr Basil Dean has made *Hassan* the most significant musical production the London stage has seen for many a day, opera not excluded. Had Flecker and Delius worked in collaboration there could hardly have been a closer spiritual affinity between the drama and the music which accompanies it. Delius has always been haunted by dreams of a far country 'beyond that last blue mountain barred with snow,' and he is never more authentically inspired than when he is singing of some Hesperides-garden, whether it be in Hy-Brasil or Samarkand, or in the island Zarathustra found beyond good and evil. This romantic element in his nature colours nearly all of the *Hassan* music, which, in spite of the limitations of form and of orchestral colour within which he has worked, is thoroughly characteristic of his mature style and an excellent initiation for those who hear Delius for the first time at His Majesty's Theatre.

Perhaps it is a little absurd to speak of limitations in connection with this music since, for all his architectural sense and mastery of the whole range of orchestral sound, some of Delius's most exquisite work has appeared in the form of short pieces for a very small orchestra — witness that perfect little poem *On hearing the first cuckoo in spring*. In *Hassan* there are several miniatures equally lovely, subtle and tender things of that magical simplicity that only a great master can achieve. Certain passages give us the very quintessence of Delius in a few bars — the little 'Street of Felicity' motif, for instance, the brief Prelude to the third act, with its beautiful use of voices singing without words as a part of the orchestra, and the entrancing Serenade which voices a passion far greater than that of the old confectioner for the fickle Yasmin.

It need hardly be said that Delius has seized upon the emotions of the drama which are universal and of no time and place — or equally of all times and all places — and given them free expression in his music unsullied by the coarse daubs of pseudo-Oriental local colour with which ninety-nine composers out of a hundred would have known no better than to bespatter them. When one thinks of the kind of music at least two very eminent British composers — both well known for their 'eastern effects' — would probably have turned out for this play, one's admiration for Mr Dean's perspicacity in selecting Delius is redoubled. There is, it is true, occasional though very sparing use of the interval of the augmented second, which is, to some ears, remotely suggestive of certain eastern scales, but it is no more characteristically eastern than our own ordinary minor scale in which it occupies so prominent a position. Indeed, if anyone will look at one or two passages in the first *Dance Rhapsody* where Delius has used it quite as extensively as in *Hassan*, he will see clearly that its association with Oriental music is purely arbitary.

Technical difficulties abound in *Hassan*, especially in the music for unaccompanied chorus behind the scenes, music of a kind which when it was first presented to certain crack north-country choirs some twelve or thirteen years ago was thought unsingable. (The particular work in question was Delius's *On Craig Ddu*, which was one of the test-pieces at the Blackpool competition festival in 1910.) But the apparent ease with which these difficulties are surmounted at His Majesty's Theatre is an eloquent testimony to the executive progress our singers have made during the last decade. Mr Eugene Goossens conducted on the first night, but much of the credit for the general excellence of the musical side of the production is due to Mr Percy Fletcher, the permanent conductor of the Theatre.

The published piano score of *Hassan* is incomplete, several numbers having been recently added at the request of Mr Dean, to meet the necessities of his production. A new edition will, however, be ready very shortly.'

Hassan — by Mrs Cecil Chesterton, from *The Bookman*, October 1923:

'The production of James Elroy Flecker's *Hassan* at His Majesty's Theatre is careful and artistic. As a spectacle it is completely satisfying. The settings, ballets, incidental music are beautiful; each picture is full of colour and movement. And having said this, one is actually conscious that the very beauty of the setting seems to depreciate the drama. As I watched the figures on a stage perfectly lit with every cunning contrivance to stimulate imagination, I was hungering for a performance shorn of its ornament in which the purpose of the poet could emerge in all its clarity. The story of the pilgrimage of Hassan, the confectioner of Bagdad, is in itself sufficiently dramatic to hold the attention. The kindly and unshapely creature, with the soul of a poet, falls in love with Yasmin, most beautiful and bitter of harlots. He sends her his choicest wares, dipped in a love philtre, by Selim, his false friend. Selim steals Yasmin for his own, and Hassan, cruelly derided, falls broken-hearted on the ground. It is in this scene that one of the loveliest of Flecker's lyrics occurs:

'How splendid in the morning glows the lily;
    with what grace he throws
His supplication to the rose . . .'

One is grateful that Delius has supplied a merely fugitive accompaniment so that the author's words lose nothing of their imagery.

The next chapter of Hassan's history is his adoption by the Caliph. Haroun al-Raschid is not the kindly ruler of legend; he uses men as an artist uses colour, painting with the red of cruelty the orange of lust. Seeking adventure, he is entertained by Rafi, King of the Beggars. Ishak, the Caliph's minstrel, desiring to meet 'sunrise on the hills,' puts the unconscious Hassan in the basket let down from Rafi's window. There follows M. Fokine's ballet of beggars and dancing girls. After which Rafi declares his intention of sacking Bagdad and nailing the Caliph alive in his coffin because the tyrant stole Pervaneh, the woman he loves.

Mr Basil Gill in this scene surmounts all the splendour of the setting. With a voice expressive of fine shades of emotion he has captured the spirit of Flecker's creation. His next appearance before the divan of the Caliph — rescued by a simple ruse of Hassan — is equally impressive. This scene is justified of its magnificence. Haroun, seated on golden cushions, is faced by the kings and potentates who owe him tribute. Against the high light — of the *Scwabe-Hasait* installation — the rich but sombre colour of their garments are symbolical. Rafi in chains and Pervaneh closely veiled are to be judged. Neither in this scene nor in the prison cell where the lovers decide whether they shall choose lifelong separation or death by torment, does Miss Laura Cowie satisfy expectation. Pervaneh is described as an ecstatic, but Miss Cowie remains devoid of any tinge of rhapsody. She is spiritually cold and when she demands that Rafi shall choose death: 'The spirits of children not yet born whisper as they crowd around us, "Endure that we may conquer",' she might be urging the cause of a society for uplift.

I am grateful to Mr Dean for his omission of perhaps the finest scene in *Hassan* — the meeting of the ghosts of Rafi and Pervaneh. Their appearance, though bathed with the most delicate phosphorescence, would have jarred. As it is we are shown but a fugitive figure flitting up the stairway, a short while since thronged with the procession of death, and hear only the cry of 'Rafi, shall we forget?' In the final scene we see Hassan, rescued from despair by Ishak, joining the pilgrims on the Golden Road to Samarkand.

Mr Henry Ainley gives a genial performance of himself rather than the confectioner of Bagdad. He plays the part at the full pitch of his voice; indeed, generally speaking, the actors are a touch too noisy. Mr Leon Quartermaine has not quite caught the author's conception of Ishak; but his delivery of certain passages suggests that he will ultimately find the true reading. Mr Edmund Willard is a superb Masrur; he moves and speaks like the historic negro of our childish terrors; and Mr Frank Cochran as Jafar, the Vizier, is excellent. Miss Cathleen Nesbitt looks very lovely, but her Yasmin is a touch too modern. The production as a whole should draw large audiences. Those who desire a spectacle will be enchanted; those who go for the sake of the play will return to the reading of the text with fresh enthusiasm.'

Hassan at His Majesty's — by J T Grein, writing in *The Sketch*, 3 October 1923:

'Flecker''s posthumous fame is, perhaps, a blessing in disguise. Had he lived, I should have apprehended for him the sad fate of Stephen Phillips — he who by some of his critics was raised to the heights of Shakespeare, Goethe, Dante, when he gave great promise in *Paolo and Francesca*, then was levelled down by his very admirers to mediocrity.

Already we have read anent *Hassan* comparisons with Shakespeare: and, dazzled by the wonderful spectacle at His Majesty's, there is no saying to what exaggeration his admirers will fly. This is no disparagement: it is an antidote to the toxin which threatens careers when clique and faction proclaim the ordainment of genius.

For *Hassan* is a beautiful play, beautiful of design and often in diction, but it is not great. You will find the like of it in many Continental literatures — in the poetic plays of France, Germany, Holland; and some of them had at least equal merits of expression, and superior qualities of structure and dramatic power. It is said, with what measure of truth I am unable to substantiate, that Flecker planned as a comedy this tale of the confectioner who for his simple device of rescuing his Caliph from the revolting King of Beggars, became a governor of three provinces, and was thrust back to his pans and his carpets. I can well believe it, for, approached with our sense of humour, we feel the comic side of phantasmagoria even in the serious scenes; and more so in the drastic representation of horrors, from the gay humour of the House of Moving Walls where the Caliph was rescued, to the horror of horrors of the pageant of protracted death — the unspeakable ordeal of two lovers who preferred one day of ecstasy, and nameless torture, to life and surrender of the woman to the harem. Satire, too, lurks under the wolf of the dramatic aspect and the harrowing proceedings. Was there not once in Russia under Catherine I a confectioner (and pastry-cook to boot), who became the Empress' lover, her lefthand ruler, the greatest man in the realm, and then, for ceasing to please his mistress, had to take, not the golden road to Samarkand, but the desolate path of eternal snows to Siberia? If there is a message in *Hassan* — and I think it transpires from the perusal of the text — it is, 'Put not your trust in princes' and 'Those in high places stand on windy planes.' To me, it is not the two love-stories — that of Hassan and the harlot, who accepts when there is something to give, who rejects when bounties are meagre; the Caliph's and the Beggar King's mortal feud for the possession of the pure Pervaneh — that constitute the value of the play. For construction is loose and the tale never moves beyond interest when unaided by scenic adornment. The charm lies in the language, mellifluous, musical, and gently seasoned with thoughts that stimulate, but are more poetically expressed than profoundly culled from life.

The illustration of the tale is Basil Dean's great work; rarely an author has had a hand so lavish and so sensitively artistic in collaboration. Dean, a disciple of Reinhardt, has learned all there was to learn from the master, and has improved his knowledge by avoiding all that is garish and cumbersome — a fault that, in later days, sometimes blurred the efforts of the younger producer. Only once has imagination stranded in stage-limitations in this production, and Dean forewarned us that it could happen. The wraiths of the departing lovers were neither impressive nor spiritually inspiring.

But, for the rest — what glorious designs, what visions of the Orient in the realistic quietude of the street where the harlot lives, in the Arabian Nights luxuriousness of palaces and revels; what sinister awe in the pageant of protracted death, intensified by Delius's macabre march heralding grimness and ill-omen; what exquisite sobriety in the march of the pilgrims to Samarkand on the red road of sand, fanned to fire by the breaking of the sun through dawn. Beautiful — beautiful — beautiful, I can only say. Unforgettable, too — that march and that pageant.

Henry Ainley was Hassan, and he was in his most romantic mood. His voice rang through the house in clarion clearness, his diction was the perfection of coinage and unctuousness. He nearly moved us in the scene when he spurned the harlot, and was conquered by her eyes. But then Miss Cathleen Nesbitt, however intense she tried to be, was not Oriental. She was of Montmartre, not of Bagdad. She did with the part what was in her power and in her personality. But the power was not magnetic, and the personality of Western allurement, not of Eastern luxury. Miss Laura Cowie, too, was not the right solution. She played with charm and an air of innocence. But in the great parting scene in prison — when terror, torture, lingering death stared her in the face, she acted but she did not vibrate. The part requires the might of a tragedienne.

Next to Ainley's, the most significant performance was the Caliph of Malcolm Keen. He was Oriental. He was all exquisite urbanity and refined cruelty. He cajoled and flayed his underlings. His was the superman playing the cat-and-mouse game with the vile thing that is man under his sway. Others deserve praise — Mr Esmé Percy, Mr Leon Quartermaine in a part of fragments, but such fragments of finesse; Mr Frank Cochrane — above all, Mr Basil Gill, grand in the ordeal of the prison scene.

Withal *Hassan* is an achievement. It eclipses *Chu Chin Chow* and *Cairo*, for poetry and fancy linked the hands of the late author and of him who became his *alter ego* — Basil Dean.'

The Stage of the Day — by Ashley Dukes. A review taken from *The Illustrated Sporting and Dramatic News*, 29 September 1923:
'James Elroy Flecker met the classical fate of the lyric poet. While he lived his work went begging, and he sold his verses for a song. He fell ill, lay for a while among the groves of Lebanon, and died in the cold sunshine of Davos, where youth winters in the bloom of health and sickness declines from summer to autumn. Now his memory is honoured, his early editions are prized, and managers give his Eastern play a setting of magnificence. When they have done their work, and done it well, the play remains the play that Flecker wrote to please himself and not to please the public; the play that grew as a tree grows, sprung from a seed of thought and nourished by the sap of fantasy. We can trace its original form of episodic conceit, the dew-draught of character, the branching inventions of intrigue, the putting forth of the sensitive shoots that form the secondary motive, the storm of cruelty and horror that shakes the boughs, the burgeoning and blossoming of the whole in the spring that blows from Samarkand. Such work must confound all dull instructors in the craft of play-making. This poet masters the stage intuitively; he has the dramatist's pair of hands. With him the art of presentation comes first. Hassan the confectioner — how likeable, how fanciful, how moving, but above all how *presentable* a character! In two minutes we know the man, in three we vow comradeship with him to the end of the tale. His modesty, his humour, his love of beauty enter into all these scenes of Bagdad, with their crumbling white walls and painted pavilions and golden palaces. The spectacle of the play itself is a procession that passes before his eyes. Simpler settings may be devised by future producers, but the presence of this character alone ensures that pageantry shall never overweight drama. He commands respect for the muse.

Hassan is fine-grained, though coarse of presence. His passion is fine-grained, though coarse of utterance. For him a soul lives in a woman behind the almond paste of flesh that the confectioner justly esteems; and if he cannot find it the woman is naught. It is a convention that the fair shall favour the prosperous and love the rich. Is it not the convention of half our entertainments? Hassan, obscure and cumbersome, is scorned by his mistress; but when he is raised to the Caliph's favour she drops a rose at his feet. The heroine of our latest musical comedy may do as much, and be little blamed for it. But to Hassan's mind the rose is poisoned. 'Last night I baked sugar, and she flung me water; this morning I bake gold, and she flings me a rose. Empty, empty, I tell you, friend, all the blue sky.' It is this same fine-grained nature that makes him rebel against the cruelties and tyrannies of the Caliphate, though his own good citizen's inclination is always to bow the knee to the Commander of the Faithful. His silence is eloquent in the trial scene when he sits at the despot's right hand. It is this nature that impels him to seek in others a passion finer than his own, and to defend it loyally — to stand sentinel over the pair of condemned lovers, to intercede for them, to protest against their torture, to forfeit all his new-won dignities, and in the end to take the 'golden road' that leads pilgrims as well as merchants away from the reeking walls of Bagdad into the open country and the unknown.

When this epic of character is unfolded on the stage, shall we talk of literature or pageantry? No, this is drama, if the word have any meaning; and the beauty of scene and music and costume is all of it treasure laid at the feet of Hassan, as the slaves of the Caliphate laid carpets and ornaments. A slovenly, unlovely figure of a man, quick in thought, slow in speech, firm in friendship, a fountain of integrity, a well of humour; he will surely live in the history of our theatre, and actors in years to come will number him among their classical parts.

Mr Ainley is the first of them. His is a good performance, sensitive, witty in manner, perhaps a thought too well-bred. Mr Leon Quartermaine is so good as Ishak, the palace poet, that one forgets that he ought to be playing the King of the Beggars, a part into which Mr Basil Gill breathes fire very well and romance very ill. Mr Esmé Percy is admirable in Selim. Elsewhere there was a good deal of miscasting, so that several excellent players in their own sphere were hard put to it to emerge with any honour but that of appearing in the play.

Mr Basil Dean and Mr Harris, his designer, have given not only their own best but their author's. Also Mr Delius and M. Fokine have found the play full of inspiration, and their rhythms have come vibrating out of it in a poetic accompaniment and dances of a tremendous plastic vigour.'

APPENDIX III

REVIEW OF THE
AMERICAN PRODUCTION

One review suffices to explain the American reception of *Hassan* in 1924, It is taken from the November edition of *The American Mercury:*
'It is not James Elroy Flecker's 'Hassan' that has failed; it is Mr Basil Dean's. Flecker wrote a play rich in the music of romance and poesy, as beautiful a thing of its kind as has appeared in recent dramatic literature; Dean staged it with all the imagination and rhythm of a sailor's smoker. The production, indeed, served as a piquant example of the low level to which the English stage, in this respect, has sunk. Dean is regarded as one of the best and most artistic of London producers. Over here, they do finer work up alleys.

I have passed an eye over seven or eight of Dean's productions, three in New York and the others in England. All of them have been drolly incompetent. Not only has the gentleman apparently no sense of the dramatic, not only is he seemingly quite innocent of the technic of projecting a manuscript over the footlights, but he is, to boot, utterly without a sense of beauty and a sense of form. His ideas of scenic investiture go back to the day when furniture was painted on the backdrop and when a "big production" was any one in which the stage was so packed and crowded with scenery and irrelevant but costly props that the actors had to make their entrances from the wings sidewise. His ideas of lighting are so absurdly antiquated that even some of the most patriotic London reviewers have difficulty in concealing their derisory hiccups. For Dean appears to believe that all that is necessary to achieve some exceptionally nobby illumination effects are a half dozen vari-colored gelatine slides supplemented by an indefatigable fellow stationed at the dimmer. And his ideas of dramatic pace are similarly reminiscent of that epoch in the theatre when scene and act intermissions were arbitrarily regulated by the time it took the candy butchers in the aisles to dispose of a sufficient number of prize packages. As the producing representative of a stage that affects loftily to look down upon our own, this Mr Dean reveals himself as a fetching bloomer. If an American producer were to put on plays as he has put on 'The Skin Game,' 'The Blue Lagoon,' 'Hassan' and so on, English critics, once they had a look at them, would burst their braces with their superior snickers.

One of the first requisites of a poetic play is a smooth and harmonious orchestration of the voices of the actors. The finest poetic drama in the world loses its effectiveness in the theatre if the rhythm, timbre and volume of such voices are not carefully regulated. If one third of the actors have French horns in their throats, another third czimbaloms, and if the third third read the lines precisely as they would read those of, say, 'Black Oxen,' the result will obviously be little more than a species of dramatic jazz. 'Hassan,' thus rehearsed by Dean's lieutenant, Mr Syndey Bland, of His Majesty's Theatre, became a number for Will Vodery's band. A second requisite of a poetic play is a scenic background that shall melt into the poetry. Dean's background was as fluid as granite. A third requisite is the achievement of an atmosphere that fitfully covers fancy and reality as with quicksilver, revealing each momentarily yet never revealing each completely — persuading the senses through a voluntary and enchanting confusion. Dean's atmosphere was that of 'Two Strangers from Nowhere.' He sought to evoke mystery with a mere blue light and romance with a pink one. In the matter of dramatic suggestion, he was equally unhappy. His scenes of melodrama were painstakingly languid; his scenes of physical passion, as, for example, the one wherein the fair Yasmin conquers the flesh of Hassan, were as sexual as playing postoffice.

Thus was a beautiful poem with its beautiful incidental music of Frederick Delius and with all its potential stage wonder reduced to nothing. The presenting company, save Murray Kinnell as the minstrel and James Dale as the caliph, showed little.

APPENDIX IV
THE LEYSIN TYPESCRIPTS

On 14 August 1913 Flecker wrote to Savery: '*Hassan* has gone off today to the typist.' He did not state how many copies had been ordered, but as carbons were used three seems a likely number. A careful perusal of Flecker's letters from this period suggests that one went to Savery and thence to Freissler for German translation; a second to Marsh, who passed it to Granville Barker; and the third to Mavrogodarto, who later handed it to Marsh in place of the copy that reached Barker, and it was this which Viola Tree read. Flecker did not retain a typed copy himself, only 'a very untidy Ms.'

It appears that he did no more work on the play before late May 1914, after his arrival at Davos. It was probably then that Dean sent him a copy of the typescript, followed by his technical recommendations, and on 2nd June Flecker wrote to Savery that he was revising *Hassan* to produce his own version for publication and the German stage, irrespective of what alterations Dean might subsequently make. At his request Savery returned the typescript which Freissler had translated so that the author could add his revisions, but although this was soon accomplished the translation was already at proof stage and they were not incorporated. On 18th June Flecker sent Dean a revised version, and it may have been this which Dean says crossed in the post with his own revision. Around September, Flecker sent Dean his second revised version, but shortly afterwards war broke out and he realised that the proposed production would have to be temporarily shelved. He therefore requested Dean to return him the latest script, but Dean was understandably reluctant to post such a valuable item abroad under war conditions, and it was December before Flecker eventually received it.   In the few weeks of life that were left to him he worked at it again, and Dean did not receive this final version until after the War had ended and Flecker had died. In the introduction to his 1951 edition Dean states that this final version 'contained numerous corrections in the first half of the play, some in Flecker's handwriting and some in that of his wife; but there were none at all in the later scenes.' He goes on to claim that the version played in the theatre in 1923 'included all the author's last-minute cuts and alterations' and that this was the text he was publishing in 1951. However, comparison with the pencil-markings in a 1922 copy used by one of the principals at the première do not bear this out. Dean continues: 'The play was first published in 1922, using Flecker's first revision.' This seems likely as it differs from both the text played at His Majesty's and the 1951 edition.

To complicate matters further the only Leysin MS known to be still in existence differs from all of these. It is housed in the Bodleian Library, Oxford, having been purchased in March 1933 'from Mrs J. E. Flecker through Mrs Harold Munro.' Again there are many alterations in the hands of both Flecker and his wife, and it can only be supposed that this is a copy other than those sent to Dean and to Messrs Heinemann. The major cuts were crossed out by a thick blue crayon, and in some instances, the changes made near the time of his death were either written in or over by his wife. The main revisions are as follows:

Act I, Scene 2: Flecker wrote at the beginning 'I should be very glad if this scene could be left exactly as it is, until the arrival of the Caliph. I cannot improve it or abridge it.' The changes he made for the Caliph's entry to the strange house meant excluding certain conditions which the voice (Host) gave him.

Act II, Scene 1: Hassan is discovered immediately in this version. Flecker changed that and cut out the Host's invitation extended to him at the opening. Beside the chorus of Culs-De-Jatte, he pencilled in brackets alongside the verse 'Show your most revolting scar' ('Perhaps a little difficult to stage!') and by the stage directions for the Ballet he wrote 'I shall raise no objection if you omit the whole ballet. The beggars can enter and range themselves to the sound of music — Then the King of the Beggars addresses them immediately.' When Rafi invites his guests to drink, Flecker wrote 'This drinking scene could be cut, but I should be sorry.' There is a change in the dialogue leading up to Rafi retelling his tale. The Caliph asked Rafi '. . . why is there blood in the fountain of your eyes when you say that word, "The Caliph"?' and it is Masrur who asks Rafi to 'Tell us the tale.' Hassan took a more active role by supporting the Caliph when he asked Rafi 'What care you for the prosperity of the people, you blind avenger?' (The character of Hassan was altered drastically after Flecker amended the first two Acts of the play, and he assumed a less forceful character. For details see Sherwood, Chapter 10).

Act II, Scene 2: Flecker made some significant changes to Yasmin's dialogue. When Ali is about to be beaten in the street below her balcony, she calls Selim to come and join her: 'Here is a man about to be beaten in the street. Praise Allah I did ever love to see a whipping . . . They have stopped beating him. Why have they stopped? He is not even bleeding. Alas, alas! I was unlucky from the womb.' Selim enquires if 'they found Uncle Hassan spitting in the fountain?', to which she replies 'Alas no: a younger man and thinner.' But Flecker only pruned her sadistic enjoyment, which did not alter her character significantly.

Act III, Scene 1:   Here he made many minor changes to dialogue, both in blue crayon and ink, but no substantial alterations to the plot.

Act III, Scene 2:   In Hassan's speech 'One of the wonderful new carpets of Ispahan' he extended the line 'O, exquisite carpet' with 'And yet . . . I hear the splash of the fountain drop by drop. Why are the flowers of the carpet that bright colour?' After Hassan had accepted the whip for 'correction' of his slaves, Flecker omitted a negro visitor who called to deliver his old carpet — the one that cost him twelve months at his Cauldron. After Hassan had said that he must visit the market, Flecker cut out his reasons:

> 'The man who would lead a spiritual existence should always have an outlet for corporal desire.'

When Yasmin was being threatened by Hassan, Flecker cut her prediction 'It is not my blood that is destined to drench this floor.'

Act III, Scene 3:   Flecker's blue crayon went through the whole of the Soldiers' song, and a great deal of Ishak's dialogue was cut. Flecker was in a hurry to finish these amendments and so have the play produced; he was also very ill and he decided to cut Selim out to reduce the plot. In the typescript Selim plays a larger part in the play. When he sees the soldiers approaching to rescue the Caliph, he panics (for no apparent reason). The next time he appears on stage he is among the beggars, who are brought on stage at the beginning of the Divan scene to receive their sentence from the Caliph. He explains to Hassan and company how he got there:

> '. . . I was a fool. They told me there was gold to win, and forced me by threats to join them.'

He begs Hassan to save him, and the Caliph makes the proposal to Hassan that 'If thou requirest this man's life, it is thine,' to which Hassan replies: 'I do not require his life of thee, O master of all lives.' The courtiers scorn Hassan but the Caliph reiterates his decision: 'He will not save thee' and so Selim dies — a move which troubles Hassan and turns him into a guilty-hero (see Sherwood, p. 209).

The exchanges of the Chief of Police and Captain of the Military with the Caliph were all prudently cut. The Chinese Philosopher, omitted in the Selim cuts, was re-inserted later. Hassan's aside as published 'But if that fountain . . .' was originally Rafi's line, to which Hassan simply asked '. . . a fountain?' Possibly Flecker gave the longer line to Hassan to include him in the scene.

Flecker cut the Caliph's interrogation of Rafi, and changed the third accusation into the major one: 'Dost thou deny that thou didst scheme this monstrous crime for the sake of a woman?' He subsequently cut the Caliph's speech 'Thou art brave.'

Act IV, Scene 1: (Not performed in London in 1923). Flecker wrote 'I at first thought of cutting out this scene entirely, but I am convinced that it must be kept (I have shortened it enormously, being not only good in itself but necessary to keep the interest in Hassan from failing).'

Selim's death is thrashed out at length by Ishak and Hassan, and the soul-searching reveals much of their characters. Hassan confesses:

'. . . This day is the first day of my exaltation, and see, I have begun it by aspiring to cut down a woman, and have ended it achieving the destruction of a man . . . I have the coward's heart . . . and in my angry vanity I have sent a man to die . . . I care not what I do for I have lost the meaning of the world. I do not know right from wrong . . .'

After they have bribed the Guards and changed into their uniforms, Hassan and Ishak then have to use force on them, as one of the guards demands to see the Caliph's pass. This dramatically weak scene was cut down but Dean did borrow part of its idea for his production, when he used Hassan and Ishak as the guards on duty in the cell, and omitted Scene 1 altogether.

Act IV, Scene 2:   Hassan, now dressed as a Guard, restrains Pervaneh from strangling Rafi, who in turn recognises him:

'He hath compassion — this guard who dropped his spear, and his face is the face of Hassan.'

Flecker omitted this rather weak episode completely. He also cut much dialogue between the lovers.

Act V, Scene 1:   Before the Caliph orders Hassan to a key position among the spectators, Flecker cut the Caliph's offer that he would spare the lovers if Hassan would die in their place. He explains

'Hassan, you are old, lonely and disgraced. They are so young, so wonderful, so handsome. Redeem your base extraction, your noble trade, your lamentable cowardice. Die and save them.'

Hassan refuses, and so for the second time he is struck with the terrible guilt complex that he hopes to purge by taking 'The golden road to Samarkand.' He asks Hassan how he got into the Cell and accuses him of giving way to

'. . . a base-born inquisitiveness to bear things which, as you say, concerned you not at all!'

For this reason he gave Hassan a place among the spectators. Before the torture began, Flecker cut the dialogue when Yasmin and Hassan encounter each other. He curses Yasmin, and his conscience remembers Selim and his fate for

'. . . I was hot in bed with thee when he was swinging in the cold . . .'

The major result of Flecker's Leysin amendments can be summarised thus: Hassan's guilty conscience is not so pronounced in the published version because the causes of his own guilt, namely Selim's death and his refusal to die in place of the lovers, have been removed.

JAMES ELROY FLECKER

James Elroy Flecker was born in London (Lewisham), on November 5th, 1884. He was the eldest of the four children of the Rev. **W. H.** Flecker, D.D., now Head Master of Dean Close School, Cheltenham. After some years at his father's school he went in 1901 to Uppingham, proceeding to Trinity College, Oxford, in 1902. He stayed at Oxford until 1907, and then came to London, teaching for a short time in Mr. Simmons' School at Hampstead. In 1908 he decided to enter the Consular Service, and went up to Cambridge (Caius College) for the tuition in Oriental languages available there. He was sent to Constantinople in June 1910, was first taken ill there in August, and in September returned to England and went to a sanatorium in the Cotswolds. He returned to his post, apparently in perfect health, in March, 1911; was transferred to Smyrna in April; and in May went on leave to Athens, where he married Miss Helle Skiadaressi, a Greek lady whom he had met in the preceding year. He spent three months' holiday in Corfu, and was sent to Beyrout, Syria, in September 1911. In December, 1912, he took a month's leave in England and Paris, returning to Beyrout in January, 1913. In March he again fell ill, and after a few weeks on the Lebanon (Brumana) he went to Switzerland, where, acting on his doctor's advice, he remained for the last eighteen months of his life. He stayed successively at Leysin, Montreux, Montana, Locarno, and (May, 1914) Davos, where on January 3, 1915, he died. He is buried in Cheltenham at the foot of the Cotswold Hills.

His published books include:—

Verse: "The Bridge of Fire" (Elkin Matthews, 1907), "Forty-two Poems" (Dent, 1911), "The Golden Journey to Samarkand" (Goschen, 1913, now published by Martin Secker) and "The Old Ships" (Poetry Bookshop, 1915).

Prose: "The Last Generation" (New Age Press, 1908), "The Grecians" (Dent, 1910), "The Scholars' Italian Grammar" (D. Nutt, 1911), and "The King of Alsander" (Goschen, 1914, now published by Allen & Unwin). He left also two unpublished Dramas "Hassan" and "Don Juan" and a number of published and unpublished short stories, articles and poems.

BASIL DEAN

It is interesting to note that it was during the period of his employment at this Theatre, under Sir Herbert Tree, that Basil Dean first came into touch with Elroy Flecker. The promise to produce "Hassan" is of nearly ten years standing; but in spite of repeated efforts it is only now that the right opportunity has been forthcoming.